THE CIVIL WAR AND INTERREGNUM
Sources for Local Historians

G. E. AYLMER AND J. S. MORRILL

THE CIVIL WAR
AND
INTERREGNUM
Sources for Local Historians

G. E. Aylmer and J. S. Morrill

Published for the
Standing Conference for Local History
by the
BEDFORD SQUARE PRESS of the
National Council of Social Service

First published 1979 by the
Bedford Square Press of the
National Council of Social Service,
26 Bedford Square,
London WC1B 3HU

ISBN 0 7199 0967 8

Printed in Great Britain by
Latimer Trend & Company Ltd
Plymouth

Contents

Foreword

This is a co-operative venture in the sense that we both contributed to the whole of the book. G. E. A. did most of the research and produced a working draft; J. S. M. devised the lay-out and wrote the second and third drafts which were subjected to joint scrutiny. But it was a co-operative venture in a wider sense. Many friends and colleagues gave willingly of their time and experience. The following were the most generous and the most put-upon: Messrs C. Elrington, W. Kellaway, C. J. Kitching, E. L. C. Mullins, K. V. Thomas, D. Smith and A. Rogers.

Among recent books, W. B. Stephens, *Sources for English Local History* (1973) has been especially useful.

Abbreviations

Add. MS	British Library Additional Manuscript
Ag. H.R.	*Agricultural History Review*
B.L. *or* B.M.	British Library *or* British Museum
B.I.H.R.	*Bulletin of the Institute of Historical Research*
Ec. H.R.	*Economic History Review*
E.H.R.	*English Historical Review*
Harl. MSS	British Library, Harleian Manuscripts
H.J.	*Historical Journal*
H.M.C.	Historical Manuscripts Commission (Strictly Royal Commission on Hist. MSS)
H.M.C. (JP)	Historical Manuscripts Commission, Joint Publications
H.M.S.O.	Her Majesty's Stationery Office
J.M.H.	*Journal of Modern History*
P.R.O.	Public Record Office
R.C.H.M.	Royal Commission on Historical Monuments

Introduction

This short book is not meant to be an exhaustive bibliography of the sources for the study of the civil war years, far less of the vast superstructure built up by successive generations of historians upon the uneven foundations constituted by those sources. Rather, we have concentrated on producing a guide to those sources peculiar to the period. It is our hope that the guide will help newcomers to research in the mid-seventeenth century to find their way around the most obvious records and that it will give them advice on how to track down the more unusual surviving ones. Two groups of people have been held particularly in mind: first, practising local historians (schoolteachers, adult education students, enthusiasts) who are turning for the first time to look at some aspect of the mid-seventeenth century; and second, the postgraduate planning to work in this area, a person familiar with secondary but not primary materials. The term 'local' has been taken to mean any part of the country smaller than a region, from a county down to the smallest administrative and social units, the parish, township, manor and household.

The pamphlet is divided into three sections. The first comments on the resources of the major depositories – local record offices, the Public Record Office, the British Library and the Bodleian Library. It gives information about what you might hope to find in these depositories and on available guides which can be consulted before making journeys to visit them. The second divides the sources into eight main subject headings and examines each in turn. After some hesitation, we abandoned our intention of following a scheme used in other bibliographies and devised one of our own. The third section consists of a series of bibliographical aids, which are intended as a very simple guide to certain groups of material and not to supplant the full bibliographical aids listed as Appendix 1 in that section. Thus, the list of recent work on the civil war is mainly a supplement to Mrs Keeler's *Bibliography of British History, Stuart Period* (1970), and the list of theses on civil war history is a personal selection and does not save students the task of searching the handlists of *Theses in Progress* and *Theses Completed* which appear annually as supplements to the *Bulletin of the Institute of Historical Research.*

I Depositories

Those wishing to study the local history of the mid-seventeenth century are likely to have to begin work in more than one place. They will certainly want to begin by exploring the resources of their local county or borough record office. But they are also likely to feel drawn towards the Public Record Office, where there is a vast array of material gathered by agencies of the central government relevant to every local community. We shall begin by looking at the principal series of documents held by each of these in turn, and will then comment on the resources of two other principal manuscript collections, those held by the British Library (formerly the British Museum) and the Bodleian Library in Oxford.

1. Local Record Offices

We must begin with a warning to those about to launch themselves into research. The natural enthusiasm at the prospect of coming to grips with the dusty relics of a bygone era must be put aside until some very tedious preparation is done. Draw up a plan of campaign by leafing through the bibliographical guides available. Look first at any published secondary works which deal with your area of research either for your own or other areas (this at least will indicate the sort of sources which are available). You can find out what these works are by consulting our appendices 3–7 and by using the bibliographical guides listed in Appendix 1. When you have drawn up a list of the sources which you know or hope exist, you will be better equipped to make your way to your local record office or the archives department of your city library. It is a good idea to write to them saying when you are coming and indicating briefly your main field of study. We can assure you of the warm and friendly welcome you can expect in most of these offices. The staff will very probably be able to add to your stock of source materials. But do not expect them to do your work for you. It is little use writing to a record office and simply asking 'What have you got on the civil war and interregnum?', or 'I am working on Upper Parsley in the 1650s, what have you got for me?'. Still less must you ask 'How many times did Oliver Cromwell sack the church at Staunch Magna?'.

County record offices were set up at different times and some are more generously funded by local authorities than others. This means that some record offices have been much better able to provide guides and indexes to their records than others. It remains true, however, that few have been able to give priority to the creation of indexes of personal names and subjects, and even indexes of place names are not often complete or up-to-date. It is therefore always best to approach the staffs initially with such queries as 'Do you have any Quarter Sessions records for this period?'; 'Have the parish registers for Longmeadow survived for this period?'; or 'Do you have any family archives which contain material for the civil war years?'. Finally, if you think there are papers that might be of use to you which are in private hands, it is always best to approach the owners through a record office. Many owners do not have the facilities to allow eager researchers into their libraries or their strong-rooms. But quite often they will be willing to allow their papers to be deposited temporarily in the record office for you to consult. There have been cases where the owners, badgered by enthusiastic researchers, have become fed-up and closed their papers to everyone. So always consult your local archivist and take his advice.

What kinds of records are kept by the local record offices? There are not many which are unique to this period. The Quarter Sessions records of the counties, corporation records and company or guild records (for the boroughs) and the parish registers for any area will normally begin before and continue after this period, and, simply because of the disruptive effects of civil war, are likely to be incomplete for the middle years of the century. The same would be generally true of other types of local administration records (constables', churchwardens' and overseers' of the poor accounts, for example) which are rarer in any case. Records relating to the new administrative instruments of the 1640s and 1650s (county committee records, papers relating to the confiscation and redemption of the goods and lands of royalists etc.) are more likely to be found in the P.R.O. and, if they survive at all in the localities, they will tend to form part of the collections of papers listed and stored as family collections.

2. The Public Record Office

The sheer volume of material in the P.R.O., covering so many fields over so long a time, means that it is even less use arriving unprepared there than at the local record office. It is simply pointless to ask the staff for general guidance on what sort of records they have. They will help you to find and use the various sorts of guides to the public records that exist, but you must tell them which series you are interested in. Above all, you must write to them in advance asking for a reader's ticket and enclosing, if at all possible, a note from your adult education teacher, supervisor or (if he knows you by then) local archivist, indicating that you are engaged on bona fide research. A similar procedure is necessary to become a reader at the British Library.

Start, as before, by using the general bibliographical guides and secondary sources to establish which series it will be worth while to investigate. Armed with this information, you can now turn to the guides issued by the P.R.O. If you are lucky you will find these in your local university library, local record office and even some large county and city libraries. If not, you will have to do the next stage of your preparation in the P.R.O. itself. Keep at your elbow the *Guide to the Contents of the Public Records* (2 vols 1963) of which Vol. I covers the law courts and Vol. II the departments of state. (A third volume, published in 1969, deals only with recent departmental transfers to the P.R.O.). Every year, H.M.S.O. produces an up-to-date list of all official record publications (these include collections in the Public Record Offices in Chancery Lane, Kew, Belfast and Edinburgh, and also in the House of Lords Record Office), whether they are in or out of print. This booklet (the most recent edition ran to eighty pages) also contains very brief introductions to each series of documents (Government Publications, Sectional List 24, *British National Archives*). With this as your companion, you can proceed from the *Guide* to the Public Record Office *Lists and Indexes* (55 vols 1892–1936, mostly reprinted in New York in the 1960s) and the *Supplementary List and Indexes* series (in progress, New York from 1964). But many of the most useful indexes and other 'finding aids' are the typed and handwritten volumes on the open shelves in the P.R.O. search rooms. Many of these have been published by the *List and Index Society* (from 1966), but many must still be consulted on the spot.

These lists and indexes vary enormously in fullness and scope. Most of them give a very brief description of the contents of each box or volume (e.g. 'letters and papers relating to sequestrations', 'order book of the committee for plundered ministers', 'certificates and receipts, Cornwall – Essex'). All of them indicate the terminal dates of the contents (e.g. 'Apr–July 1643', '1647–1653', 'mainly seventeenth century'), and where appropriate the guides usually indicate if the contents relate to a particular part of the country. These guides will thus help you to discover which call numbers in any given series may contain information relevant to you. They simply reduce the size of the academic haystacks in which you must seek your needles.

For most people, the starting-point will be the State Papers series, and a brief description of the contents of the main groups of documents for this period (SP, series 16–28) is given as Appendix 2. For some of these series, there are full calendars which summarise the contents of each document. For the years 1640–60 the most important are the *Calendar of State Papers Domestic, Charles I* (vols XVI–XXIII 1640–49) and *The Commonwealth* (13 vols 1649–60) which cover far more ground than their predecessor-volumes. The previous (and subsequent) volumes of *Calendars of State Papers Domestic* consisted of the papers of successive Secretaries of State, which still form part of the calendars. But in addition the calendars contain full summaries of the papers received and despatched by the most powerful of all the parliamentary committees during the civil war, the so-called Committee of Both Kingdoms 1644–7 (later, after the withdrawal of the Scots, renamed the Derby House Committee, 1647–9), and also the books of successive Councils of State from 1649–60. In general the originals add little to the *Calendars*, but some cross-checking may be desirable. The indexes of the calendars are far from infallible, particularly in respect of place names, and should be used with care.

The calendar of two of the other committees created during the civil war to raise money for the parliamentary cause, the *Calendar of the Committee for Compounding with Delinquents* 1643–60 (5 vols 1888–93), and the *Calendar of the Committee for the Advance of Money* 1643–56 (3 vols 1888) both summarise the letter and order books of these committees and also pull together entries referring to individuals summoned before them. In the case of the Compounders who levied fines from royalists, the calendar contains entries for every individual concerned, and lists all the volume and folio numbers relating to his case. But the entries themselves are often inadequate and should be taken as a necessary guide to the full contents of the originals. The *Committee for the Advance of Money* levied money from all those who had failed to lend money voluntarily to Parliament but the calender of its proceedings is much weaker since it is selective and contains no guide within it to the uncalendared part. Reference must be made back to the relevant *List and Index*. Since many of the original volumes are in fact arranged geographically, the calendar can serve to alert you to likely concentrations of material. It is our experience that the indexes of the calendars are excellent for persons and reasonable but not infallible for places (individual townships or manors are well done, but general county entries are variable). In addition, you might find material of use in the *Calendar of State Papers Venetian* (which contains reports from various parts of the country). Indeed the great strength of all these series is that they do contain a vast number of reports from the localities to the central government, and any student of military, political or administrative history should make the study of these calendars an early priority. It will also be worth while for students of economic, ecclesiastical and educational history to look at these records to witness the fortunes of institutions and individuals in their area of study. Copies of these calendars are fairly widely scattered throughout England and most students ought to be able to find copies within twenty or thirty miles of their home.

Harvester Press have undertaken a bold venture which deserves success. They are preparing reels of microfilm of unpublished and uncalendared items from the state papers for the period 1640–60. The project consists of five parts, each of which is accompanied by an introductory pamphlet. The introduction to the first part is itself a useful guide to the administrative structure of the 1640s and can be read with profit even if the microfilms themselves are not to be used. The first series consists mainly of letter or order books of various parliamentary committees for the 1640s such as the Committee for Sequestrations (SP20), the Committee for Plundered Ministers (SP22), the Committee of Indemnity (SP24), together with a series of items from the SP28 series, including papers relating to the provision of wood and fuel to London, accounts books of the Treasurers at War, Papers of the Committee for Taking the Accounts of the Kingdom and of the Committee of Petitions. The second, third and fourth parts consist of records relating to the sale and disposal of Crown properties during the Interregnum. Part two contains the surveys of the Crown lands arranged county by county (E317). They include full details of rent, entry fines, manorial customs, the duties and privileges claimed by various classes of tenants, as well as acreages and details of the demesne and free-holds. The third and fourth parts give details of the purchasers of Crown lands (third part) and of fee farm rents (fourth part). They are again arranged by county (E121, E308, E320). The fifth part contains several classes of financial record: (a) military accounts, (b) documents illustrating exchequer procedure, (c) ecclesiastical records, specifically the mulcting of recusants and of first fruits and tenths from ministers new to their livings and (d) a few records of Exchequer judicial procedure in suits between individuals. The microfilms are generally easy to use and although they all relate to the work of committees at the centre, almost every aspect of local history is covered by these documents. If you can find a library which has invested in this series, you could save yourself a lot of time and expense in journeys to London. The full title of the venture is *Unpublished State Papers of the English Civil War and Interregnum*. It is under the editorial direction of Michael Hawkins.

The state papers are the series of central government records most affected by the events of the period. Most of the other series continue, though in a modified form. The common law courts, the Court of Chancery and the Assizes all resumed after the civil war. The Exchequer resumed its control of most of the financial business, and the key series for local historians, the lay subsidies amongst the King's Remembrancer Rolls, continue to exist. But whereas these rolls had previously listed all those liable to pay subsidies to the Crown, they are now arranged to show yields from each hundred or town rather than from individuals. One of the disadvantages for the historian of the change to the new direct levy, the 'assessment', was that this required the raising of a stated amount from the country every month, rather than being at a rate of so much in the pound (i.e. the government determined the total sum it required, and divided this amount between the counties; local commissioners divided this up between hundreds and parishes, and constables assessed individuals). Under this new system, the government was uninterested in the burden on individuals; its controls were over geographical units only. Unhappily, virtually no constables' assessment lists have survived.

The collapse of the ecclesiastical courts produced new arrangements for proving wills. They were handled nationally by a special probate court. However, at the Restoration the records were taken over by the ecclesiastical courts and are now listed in the same series as the pre-1640 wills. The relevant volumes are Probate 10 (surviving wills), and Probate 11 (registers); the latter series has now normally to be consulted on microfilm (reading machines are available in the search room).

The public records are daunting. These are now divided between the old, Victorian-built P.R.O. in Chancery Lane (London WC2A 1LR) and the new, 1970s one at Kew (Ruskin Avenue, Kew, Richmond, Surrey TW9 4DU). The records are split by classes of documents and not by date. Most series of importance for the years 1640–60 are still in central London. Those at Kew which the local historian might wish to consult are: Admiralty (ADM) but *not* High Court of Admiralty (HCA); Exchequer and Audit Department (AO) but *not* Exchequer (E); Treasury (T); and War Office (WO), which includes the Ordnance Office. There are more problems for the users of Chancery Lane than anywhere else. But we may have made it sound more difficult than it actually is. Keep a clear head, a copy of the *Guide to the Contents of the Public Record Office* by your elbow, and all should be well.

3. The British Library

Quite apart from the facilities afforded in the main reading room and North Library for the study of printed books of all periods, most students will find important collections relevant to their area of study in the manuscript department of the British Library. The logic of their system of cataloguing manuscripts is a purely historical one. Several huge and artificial collections have retained their independent integrity and even their initial internal organisation (the Cottonian MSS are still listed by the name of the Roman emperor's bust which sat over each bookcase in Sir Robert Cotton's library in the early seventeenth century!). Separate catalogues exist for the Cottonian, Harleian, Sloane, Lansdowne, Stowe and Hargrave collections, although none has an adequate index. In general they offer brief descriptions of the type of documents in each volume, the time-span covered by them and (if relevant) the locality with which the volume as a whole is concerned.

From these published catalogues, which can be found in some good local libraries, you can turn to the Additional MSS. These are the many collections which the Museum has collected by gift or purchase over the last two centuries. They are an open series, each with a call number corresponding to its date of acquisition by the library. The series now contains more than 60,000 items, exclusive of the Egerton series. There is a brief description of each volume in the huge *Catalogue of Additions to the Manuscripts in the British Museum*. The publication of this catalogue has only reached items acquired before 1946. However, the Department of Manuscripts keeps typed lists which bring the catalogue up to date, and the List and Index Society are publishing these in their additional series. The catalogues contain indexes of persons and places. For the 'Rough Register' of Acquisitions from 1961 to 1975, see *List and Index Society, Special Series* (vols 7, 8, 10, 1974/5/7).

There are only two ways to use the records held in the manuscripts department of the British Library. One is to go along there armed with a list of call numbers culled from general reading and from browsing through general works; the other is to go through the catalogues page by page. This is a long and tedious business but can lead on to exciting discoveries.

For the civil war period, all the collections (Additional, Harleian and Sloane in particular) contain every kind of record: many important taxation records, official accounts books, even county committee and central committee order and letter books. This sometimes came about because the civil servants treated their public papers as though they were their own and placed them in their family muniments. But quite frequently they were simply misappropriated by later antiquaries for their own edification. Thus, Randle Holme of Chester offered, in the later seventeenth century, to sort out the city archives and put them in order, and then took the opportunity to keep some of the most interesting items for himself. His collection later passed to Robert Harley and from him to the British Museum. As a consequence of Holme's questionable action, the series of Cheshire sequestration papers and accounts which he misappropriated are the fullest to survive. Several important series of official royalist papers also survive (see below). Genealogy and military history are well served. In general the political, administrative and military historian will find most for himself, the social, economic and demographic historian least. But probably the greatest bulk of material lies in the dozens of boxes and books of private letters which survive, particularly in Additional MSS. This is the greatest single collection of private letters in existence, the excitements scattered though they are amidst a great many dull and commonplace items.

In the North Library, beyond the main reading room, you can study one of the most important of all printed collections: the so-called Thomason Tracts, the 20,000 newspapers and pamphlets collected by a London bookseller and publisher from 1640 to 1661. These too must normally now be read on microfilm, on reading machines in the Library. George Thomason seems to have got hold of 95 per cent of all publications of these years, and they are fundamental to our knowledge of the politics, religion, military history and economic conditions of the period. There is a two-volume *Catalogue of The Pamphlets, Books, Newspapers, and Manuscripts collected by George Thomason 1640–1661* (eds G. K. Fortescue and others), which is a chronological list with a good index of places as well as of persons and topics. This is the period which saw the first true flowering of the English newspaper and also a deluge of pamphleteering. The importance of this collection, made at a time when there was no effective censorship of the production or distribution of newspapers (the royalist diurnals were freely available in London throughout the war) cannot be exaggerated. The Thomason catalogue is an excellent one. But two points are worth noting. First, the newspapers in Thomason are bound up chronologically, all the newspapers for one week (together with the pamphlets of the day) being kept together. It is not easy to get a run of a particular paper over a long period. If you want to study the events of a particular period, go to Thomason; but they are rather less useful for events outside London. If you want to study the development of a particular viewpoint (e.g. the Leveller programme in *The Moderate*), it may be easier for you to go to one of the other collections with extensive newspaper holdings organised in runs of the same diurnal. For the parliamentarian papers, see above all the runs in the Clarke collection at Worcester College, Oxford. Secondly, the Thomason holdings of royalist papers are less complete than those at the Bodleian Library, or the Library of Corpus Christi College, Oxford.

4. The Bodleian Library

Superficially, the organisation is very similar to that of the British Library department of manuscripts. There is an open series of literary and historical Manuscripts (the Western MSS) which is constantly added to by new acquisitions, and there are autonomous collections catalogued separately, of which those with the most mid-seventeenth century items are the Ashmole, Gough, Carte, Rawlinson and Tanner collections. Some of these are of fundamental importance like the volumes of letters received by William Lenthall, speaker of the Long Parliament (Tanner MSS 66–51 – so described because they are in reverse chronological order). The Bodleian is both worse and better than elsewhere in its aids to researchers. *The Summary Catalogue* of Western MSS (7 vols – 8 parts 1895–1953) with the more recent additions in typescript are easy to use and have excellent cross-references. The important *Clarendon State Papers* (within the Western MSS) have now been splendidly calendared with a fine index (5 vols Oxford 1872–1970). But for other collections, above all the Carte MSS which contain many (mainly ecclesiastical) records of the mid-seventeenth century, there is only a handwritten catalogue kept in the Library itself. Once again, the researcher will find a wealth of private letters and diaries, but also volumes of official papers and accounts etc. which have strayed from the straight and narrow road which leads to the P.R.O. in Chancery Lane. (For guides to other manuscript collections, see Appendix 1.)

Among other outstanding collections, of far more than local interest but with materials relevant for many localities are: the National Library of Scotland and the Scottish Record Office in Edinburgh; the National Library of Wales in Aberystwyth; the Public Record Office of Northern Ireland in Belfast; and the Cambridge University Library. For the addresses, phone numbers, opening hours, etc., of all record offices, see The Royal Commission on Historical Manuscripts, *Record Repositories in Great Britain* (6th edn 1979).

Since we went to press, a selection from the Tanner MSS, including all the Lenthall Papers (Tanner vols 66–51) has appeared in a microfilm edition, published by Harvester Press.

II Topics

1. Population and Social Structure

The basic source for this, as for all periods between the Reformation and the nineteenth century, is the registers of births, marriages and deaths made and kept locally. But on the whole, such registers were worse kept during the civil war and interregnum than either before 1640 or after 1660. The disruptive effects of civil war, political atrophy and the disintegration of the parochial system, all made for less effective record-keeping. Two other factors made the preservation of records less likely. Before and after these dates, duplicates of the parish registers were sent off to diocesan officials, and historians can turn to these bishops' transcripts for lacunae in parochial records. Such duplicates were not made between 1641 and 1660. Secondly, in 1653, the Barebones Assembly enacted that in future the registration of births, marriages and deaths should be undertaken by civilians appointed by the justices rather than by the clerk of each parish. At Easingwold in Yorkshire, the incumbent drily recalled, 'the Keeping of the Register being put into the hands of those who are termed laymen by such as had no good will to the ministry (1653) was afterwards made void, restored and continued as followeth, 1659 . . .'. Perversely, he destroyed the 1653-9 civil registers, and it seems probable that his action was followed by other incumbents. However, in some areas the parish clerk did continue to act as civil registrar (e.g. Leeds). At Stamford, all six parishes were served by one lay 'Register'. So all the normal cautions about using the registers for demographic analysis or family reconstitution apply with special force. The uncontrolled spread of chapels outside the parochial system may also have affected registration.

The disruptions of war, and the collapse of the ecclesiastical courts, mean that far fewer wills have survived for the period 1642-52. The situation improves dramatically, however, for the years after 1652 when the Commonwealth established lay Judges of Probate. In fact for the period 1649–60 the records are easier to use than for any other period before recent times, since virtually all wills were proved nationally, and the records were re-absorbed into those of the Prerogative Court of Canterbury in 1660. They are all preserved at the Public Record Office. The relevant call numbers are Prob. 10 (surviving original wills), Prob. 11 (register books of wills), and Prob. 12 (finding aids on the open shelves). See also Prob. 8/42 (Probate Act Book) and Prob. 6/234 (Act Book for wills proven at Oxford during the royalist occupations, 1642–6). For published aids, see (eds) J. and G. F. Matthews, *Abstracts of Probate Acts in the Prerogative Court of Canterbury*, vols IV–VII (1905–11) for the years 1640–52, then 'Index of Wills', *British Rec. Soc.*, *Index Library* (vol. 54, part VII, 1653–6, and vol. 61, part VIII, 1657–60) and 'Index to Administrations' (*ibid.* vols 72, 74 and 75, part V, 1655–60). All references in the above are to the call numbers which prevailed when the originals were kept in Somerset House. Their P.R.O. references can only be established in the search-room itself. Of course many of the individuals who were active during these years died after 1660. Indexes of P.C.C. wills have now been published down to 1700 (see J. H. Morrisson, *Prerogative Court of Canterbury: Wills, Sentences and Probate Acts 1661–70 (Inclusive)* (1935); B.R.S., *Index Library* (vols 67, 71, 77 and 80). For others see A. J. Camp, *Wills and their Whereabouts* (1963) or J. S. W. Gibson, *Wills and Where to Find Them* (B.R.S. 1974).

One series of records unique to the period affords an opportunity to examine the wealth and possessions of many men of great or middling fortunes. These are the records of the Committees of Compounding (SP23) and Sequestrations (SP20). During the civil war, parliament took powers to 'sequester', that is to seize the personal possessions and real property of all 'delinquents', both royalists and catholics. The moveable goods were to be inventoried and sold, the landed property leased for the profit of the state. Most royalists and non-combatant catholics were subsequently allowed to 'compound', that is to have their lands restored in return for the payment of a fine expressed as a fraction of the capital value of the property. The papers of these committees thus contain estimates of the capital value of a great many estates, inventories of personal estates and rent rolls and other estate documents. All these are difficult to use because of the 'delinquent's' opportunity to undervalue his lands or to conceal some of them, and because they often reflect short-term dilapidations occasioned by the war. Perhaps most important, however, is the vast amount of information about marriage contracts, dower rights, annuities for younger sons, etc. which were deductible from the pre-composition assessment in certain circumstances. The best approach to these documents is through the biographical entries in the *Cal. Committee for Compounding*, which should not be treated as exhaustive. The original papers (unlike the calendar) are to some extent arranged geographically, and a short analysis of the calendar will tell you which volumes of the original papers contain most for your area.

The use of tax records for these purposes is likewise subject to the usual cautions. The most important would have been the records of the Poll Taxes of 1641 and 1660. But they have survived for few areas. For what there is, see the lists of the Exchequer, King's Remembrancer, lay subsidy Rolls (P.R.O. series E.179) in the *List and Index Society* (vols 44, 54, 63, 75, 87). The parliamentarian weekly pay (later the monthly assessment) 1643–60 was collected locally according to the traditional methods employed for local rates, and very few records listing the contributions of individuals have survived. The handful of cases known to us all relate to the boroughs and are mostly in the local record offices.

Much fuller, but problematical to use, are the Prostestation returns of 1641–2. It was intended that all males over sixteen years of age should take this oath, but it was so worded that few catholics would in practice do so. The thoroughness with which it was applied is open to doubt. But there are signs that a serious effort was made in some areas to enforce it rigorously. Thus a return from Wollaton parish in Nottinghamshire was glossed with the words 'there is not any person within this parish that hath refused the protestation'. The extensive surviving returns are all in the House of Lords Record Office (see the list in H.M.C., *5th Report*, appendix, pp. 3, 120–34). They have been printed for all or part of Dorset, Durham, Halifax, Huntingdonshire, Oxfordshire, Sussex and Westmorland by the appropriate local record societies, and for parts of Middlesex by (ed.) A. J. C. Guimaraens, *British Archivist*, supplement 1 (1913–20), and (ed.) S. A. J. McVeigh, *W. Drayton & District Historian* (vol. XXXI, 1969). This series both adds to, and provides a cross-check on, other demographic or genealogical evidence.

The genealogist is not much helped by the records for this

period, since there were no heralds' visitations between 1634–62, though Richard Cromwell planned one in 1659 (*Cal. St. Pap. Dom.*, 1658–9, pp. 291–2). There are some references, however, in A. Wagner, *English Genealogy* (2nd edn, 1972), a book which dispels the view of genealogy as mere snobbish ancestor-hunting, and shows its connection with social history. Some of the sources listed in the following sections (particularly 3–4) are, however, also useful for students of demographic and social history; the parliamentary surveys of the 1650s in particular are often of great value. See J. Thirsk, 'Sources of Information for Population, 1500–1760', *The Amateur Historian*, vol. 4, parts 4 and 5 (1959); and more generally see also (eds) D. V. Glass and D. E. C. Eversley, *Population in History: Essays in Historical Demography* (1965; paperback edn 1974); (ed.) G. R. Elton, 'The Sources of History: Studies in the Use of Historical Evidence', T. H. Hollingsworth, *Historical Demography* (1969); (ed.) E. A. Wrigley, *An Introduction to English Historical Demography, From the 16th to the 19th Century* (1966) and the periodical *Local Population Studies* (note its special supplement, *The Plague Reconsidered: A New Look at its Origins and Effects in 16th and 17th-century England*, L.P.S. 1977).

2. Economic History

(a) Industry, trade and communications
The sources for the economic history of the mid-seventeenth century are little different from those for other parts of the early modern period. However, fewer of them have been published, since a self-perpetuating convention has led most economic historians to terminate their studies at 1640 or begin them at 1660. This makes the study of the middle years of the century one of the most potentially exciting. On the one hand, the civil wars disrupted communications and trade, and inhibited investment in manufacturing by inaugurating unprecedented government demand for cash, while at the same time releasing an enormous quantity of Crown, church and royalist land for cheap sale. On the other, the great expansion of government demand for metal goods (weapons, etc.), cloth (uniforms, etc.) and leather (shoes, etc.) must have stimulated production in some areas. Work on these subjects has hardly begun. Even the best general surveys largely ignore the purely economic effects of the

civil wars. See L. A. Clarkson, *The Pre-Industrial Economy in England* (1971), D. C. Coleman, *The Economy of England, 1450–1750* (1976) which have excellent bibliographies; C. Wilson, *England's Apprenticeship 1603–1763* (1965), C. Hill, *Reformation to Industrial Revolution* (1967) (not one of his best books). The best starting-point may well be (eds) J. Thirsk and J. P. Cooper, *17th Century Economic Documents* (1973). This contains no notes or commentary, but does indicate the sorts of sources which are available.

One difficulty with this subject is the lack of a solid core of documents around which to work. The clothing industry for example can be studied in some areas from guild records, the papers of clothiers, inventories, wills etc.; in others it has to be pieced together from the legal records, from the administrative activity of the J.P.s recorded in quarter sessions papers, from parliamentary debates and the demand for local acts. In this area more than any other, the starting-point must be the secondary literature. Trace the most relevant studies through the bibliographical aids available (Appendix 1, items 6 and 7, Clarkson *op. cit*) and look at three other surveys of the period: J. P. Cooper's chapter and bibliography in (ed.) G. E. Aylmer, *The Interregnum* (1972); M. Ashley, *Financial and Commercial Policy Under the Cromwellian Protectorate* (1934, reprinted 1962); and M. James, *Social Problems and Policy during the Puritan Revolution* (1930, reprinted 1966).

Some source materials are easily available. For two different groups of investors (not grouped regionally), see T. K. Rabb, *Enterprise and Empire* (Harvard U.P. 1967) and K. S. Bottigheimer, *English Money and Irish Land* (1971). Business records generally are explored and surveyed in three articles by Grassby and two by Coleman: R. Grassby, 'The Personal Wealth of the Business Community', *Ec. H.R.*, 23 (1970); 'English Merchant Capitalism . . .', *Past and Present*, 46 (1970); and 'The Rate of Profit in 17th-Century England', *E. H.R.*, 84 (1969). D. Coleman, 'Sir John Bankes . . .' in (ed.) F. J. Fisher, *Essays . . . in Honour of R. H. Tawney* (1961), and 'London Scriveners and the Estate Market . . .', *Ec. H.R.*, 4 (1951–2).

Certain special problems relating to the history of seaports and coastal areas generally may conveniently be bracketed with the local aspects of seaborne trade and shipping. These include the Navy and naval warfare, smuggling, ship-building and dockyards, the fisheries and the salt industry. A great deal of incidental material can be culled from the relevant volumes in the SP18 series (*Lists and Indexes* 43, calendared as part of the *Cal. State Papers Domestic*). Some idea of the extent to which the ordinary record series for trade at the ports was disrupted for the 1640s and 1650s may be gauged from (ed.) N. J. Williams, P.R.O., *Descriptive List of Queen's Remembrancer, Port Books, I,* 1565–1700 (1960). For legal problems and local cases see 'Records of the High Court of Admiralty', *List and Index Society,* 27 (1967). For local aspects of the Navy and naval warfare, see (eds) J. R. Powell and E. K. Timings, 'Documents Relating to the Civil War 1642–8', *Navy Rec. Soc.,* 105 (1963), and other volumes in the series (e.g. (eds) S. R. Gardiner and C. T. Atkinson, 'Letters and Papers relating to the First Dutch War', *Navy Rec. Soc.,* 13, 17, 30, 37, 41, 66 (1899–1930); (ed.) A. C. Dewar 'Corrections . . .' to the same, *Navy Rec. Soc.* (1931).

For the records of a particular port, see (ed.) H. E. Nott, 'The Deposition Books of Bristol, I, 1643–7', *Bristol Rec. Soc.,* 6 (1935); (ed.) H. E. Nott, *ibid.,* 'Vol. II, 1650–4', 13 (1948); (ed.) P. McGrath, 'Records relating to the Society of Merchant Adventurers of Bristol in the 17th Century', *ibid.,* 17 (1952); (ed.) P. McGrath, 'Merchants and Merchandise in 17th century Bristol', *ibid.,* 19 (1955).

A category of town record more often used by historians of the later middle ages, but valuable for the interregnum, is best represented by (ed.) A. L. Merson, 'A Calendar of Apprenticeship Registers, 1609–1740', *Southampton Rec. Soc.,* 12 (1968); and (ed.) A. Daly, 'Kingston-upon-Thames Register of Apprentices 1563–1713', *Surrey Rec. Soc.,* 28 (1974).

Above all the economic historian should not hesitate to dip into the Commonwealth Exchequer Papers (SP28, see Appendix 2). Many of the orders and warrants of the army committee and county committees relate to the settlement of military purchases and requisitions of manufactured goods. The absence of local studies of trade and industry during the civil war and interregnum does not mean the task is impossible. For those with patience and stamina, the rewards could be great.

(b) Agriculture: the ownership, tenure and use of land

Those sources and modern studies which are specific to the 1640s and 1650s relate largely to the land sales and confiscations of the years 1646–53. Before plunging into the sources it is best to note recent studies. Among the most important are H. J.

Habakkuk, 'Public Finance and the Sale of Confiscated Property during the Interregnum', *Ec. H.R.*, 15 (1962); 'Landowners and the Civil War', *Ec. H.R.*, 18 (1965); and 'Parliamentary Army and Crown Lands', *Welsh History Review* (1971); I. Gentles, 'The Management of Crown Lands', *Ag. H.R.* (1971) and 'The Sale of Crown Lands', *Ec. H.R.*, 26 (1973); and debate between M. Kishlansky and I. Gentles in *Ec. H.R.*, 29 (1976); J. Thirsk, 'The Sales of Royalist Land', *Ec. H.R.*, 5 (1952); P. G. Holiday, 'Land Sales and Repurchases in Yorkshire, 1643–1665', *Northern History*, 5 (1970); B. G. Blackwood, *The Lancashire Gentry and the Great Rebellion*, chapter 4 (1978). See also Appendix 8, items 1, 3, 5. Professor Gentles and Sir John Habakkuk are both preparing studies of the sales of Bishops' lands, and Gordon Blackwood's recent study of Lancashire in the 1640s and 1650s (Chetham Society) contains an important study of land sales there. No one has yet tackled the Dean and Chapter lands.

The sources for changes in landownership and the investigations which often accompanied these changes are largely in the Public Record Office. First there are the chancery Close Rolls (C.54) which record transfers of land (contemporary index in the Long Room at the P.R.O.); Common Pleas, Feet of Fines (C.P.25, contemporary index in the Round Room, Index, 17238–40); Exchequer, Depositions by Commission (E134) – for which there is a calendar for the reign of Charles I in the *Appendix to the 39th Report of the Deputy Keeper of the Public Records*, and for the years 1649–60 in the *Appendix to the 40th Report*. . . . The main additional source for these years is the so-called 'parliamentary surveys' of church property in the early 1650s (Chancery C94 series). The surveys exist for twenty-one English counties, and a list is kept in the Round Room; for Surveys of the Duchy of Lancaster estates (scattered over many counties), see the D.L.32 series (*Lists and Indexes* 14) and J. Houston, *A Catalogue of Ecclesiastical Records . . . 1643–1660* pp. 88–195, which lists the surveys of church lands kept at Lambeth. For those surveys which have been printed, see Appendix 6. For fee-farm rents, see also *List and Index Soc.* (1967), Augmentation Office Miscellaneous Books (E315). There is further material on the disposal of fee-farm rents and of the Crown Lands proper in SP26 (see Appendix 2). The purchasers of bishops' lands are clearly set out in tabular form in Bodleian Library, MS Rawlinson B.239. For all categories of survey, see

S. C. Newton's article in *History*, 53 (1968). For Crown lands see p. 8 above.

Individual deeds, indentures, mortgages, leases, trusts etc. are of course widely scattered for these years as for other periods, and their survival is haphazard. Large collections exist in most county record offices, though few have been able to produce guides or indexes. Those for 1652-60 have the advantage, like other legal documents of those years, of being in English and in 'normal' handwriting, not court hand – one of the few concessions of the Rump to radical demands. But the records of the royalists under sequestration should not be ignored. These often include rentals, and certainly contain a great deal of information about mortgages and marriage settlements. The records of some central committees (SP20, SP23, see Appendix 2) are a good starting point. But try to find the accounts books of the local collectors or agents of the sequestrators. Many of these are in the SP28 series (particularly volumes 205-18) but many have strayed into other collections (a magnificent series for Cheshire is in the Harleian MSS in the British Library). On the vexed question of enclosures, see W. E. Tate, *The English Village Community and the Enclosure Movement* (1967). For the royal forests, a special category of Crown lands, see a case study, P. A. J. Pettit, 'The Royal Forests of Northants ... 1558-1714' *Northants Rec. Soc.*, 23 (1968). For some good recent examples of what can be done to reconstruct the economy and social structure of village communities, see W. G. Hoskins, *Essays in Leicestershire History* (1950), *The Midland Peasant* (1957)—on Wigston Magna; *Provincial England* (1963); J. Thirsk, *English Peasant Farming* (1957)—on Lincolnshire; D. G. Hey, *An English Rural Community* (1974)—on Myddle in Shropshire; M. Spufford, *Contrasting Communities* (1974)—on Cambridgeshire; A. Macfarlane with S. Harrison and C. Jardine, *Reconstructing Historical Communities* (1977)—on Earls Colne in Essex and Kirby Lonsdale in Cumbria; and V. Skipp, *Crisis and Development* (1978) on the Forest of Arden.

(c) Poor relief, charities, prices and wages

Most of the sources here are similar to those for the years before 1640 and after 1660, but they are, on the whole, less complete. Thus, the starting points will be in the quarter sessions records, particularly the order books (and, to a less extent, in the assize records), and also amongst the parish records, in the overseers' and churchwardens' accounts. A good recent introductory survey of the history of poor relief, which is at its strongest in pointing out the difficulties in handling these sources, is G. Oxley, *Poor Relief in England and Wales 1601–1834* (1974). Some useful general works span the interregnum, e.g. E. M. Hampson, *The Treatment of the Poor in Cambridgeshire, 1597–1834* (Cambridge 1934); others deal more exclusively with these years, e.g. M. James, *Social Problems and Policy during the Puritan Revolution* (1930, reprinted 1966) especially chapter 6; A. L. Beier, 'Poor Law in Warwickshire, 1630–1660', *Past & Present*, 35 (1966). For examples of local records, see (ed.) E. Melling, 'The Poor', *Kentish Sources*, IV (Maidstone 1964), and Hampshire Archivists Group, *Poor Law in Hants through the Centuries* (1970). Whether or not one accepts the validity of his methods, and hence his conclusions, there is much material on private efforts to ameliorate charity in works by Jordan. See W. K. Jordan, *Philanthropy in England 1480–1660* (1959), *The Charities of Rural England* (1960), *The Charities of London* (1960), Monographs on Bristol and Somerset in *Trans. American Phil. Soc.*, 50/8 (1960), on Kent (*Archaeologia Cantiana*, 65 (1961)), and on Lancashire (*Chetham Soc.*, 9 (1962)). Also useful are *Lists and Indexes* 10, 'A List of Proceedings of Commissions of Charitable Uses' (since 1601), and G. Jones, *History of the Law of Charity* (1969).

There are several sources from which the history of prices and wages can be tracked down. See J. E. Thorold Rogers, *History of Agriculture and Prices in England*, vols 5 and 6 (1898–1900); *Six Centuries of Work and Wages* (1884); W. H. Beveridge *et al.*, *Prices and Wages in England from the 12th to the 19th Centuries*, vol. 1 (1939); E. H. Phelps-Brown and S. Hopkins, series of articles in *Economica* (1955–8), reprinted in (ed.) E. M. Carus-Wilson, *Essays in Economic History*, vols 2–3 (1962). One particular source, the wage assessments fixed by the J.P.s under the terms of the statute of artificers (1563) are fully listed and discussed in (ed.) W. E. Minchinton, *Wage Regulations in Pre-Industrial England* (1972), especially in the introduction, appendix A and bibliography. Despite this and other works, there is much unused source material, and good work remains to be done in this field.

3. Local Government

This has been the great 'growth sector' among historians in recent years, but there is still much to be done. It is true that it is this topic for which the surviving materials will vary most from one county to another, but no one who has hunted assiduously for materials for his or her town or county has failed to turn up interesting material. Remember how the texture of local government thickened in these years. Most of the old institutions were revived after being disrupted by the civil war: quarter sessions, assizes, borough assemblies and courts. But overlaying them were entirely new structures. Parliament devised a system of committees to handle problems of security, finance and military organisation. In some counties a single all-purpose committee evolved; in others each function was dealt with by different men. In some countries effective power devolved upon sub-committees in each hundred, lathe etc.; in others the county committees retained control. Many counties were grouped together into 'associations' and sometimes the records of committees of the associations have survived. For an analysis of this intricate pattern, and for comments on the arrangements in many counties, see J. S. Morrill, *The Revolt of the Provinces* (1976), part 2. For a list of the printed quarter sessions material, see below, Appendix 3; for printed borough records, Appendix 4; for printed county committee papers, Appendix 5.

In general, the work of committees in respect of sequestrations, finance and general administration has survived most commonly. The activities of committees with regard to the militia are much less well known and there is no known committee book to match the best of the several sets of lieutenancy papers for the previous period. Anyone finding such a book or collection would have a scoop indeed. The records for committees in the 1640s and 1650s ignored traditional borough rights and jurisdictions, and subjected the towns to county control. Thus for the fate of urban royalists, for the levying of money etc., students must turn to the relevant county records. For those few towns (the number varied between eighteen and twenty-six) permitted to retain a committee structure distinct from that of the counties in which they stood, students should turn to the various assessment ordinances printed in (eds) C. H. Firth and R. S. Rait *Acts and Ordinances of the Interregnum*, 3 vols (1911, reprinted Florida 1972, Abingdon 1979).

For the counties the prospects are better. A guide to published and unpublished quarter sessions records is given below as Appendix 3. The best guide to the composition of commissions of the peace is T. G. Barnes and A. Hassell Smith 'Justices of the Peace from 1558–1688; a Revised list of Sources' *B.I.H.R.*, XXXII (1959), pp. 221–42. But for Welsh counties, see now a complete list of J.P.s for the period in (ed.) J. R. S. Phillips *The Justices of the Peace in Wales and Monmouthshire 1541–1689* (Cardiff, 1975).

The half-yearly Assizes, when the common law judges visited the shires to deal with the more serious felonies, etc. and to act as a central government advisory service and inspectorate, continued throughout the period, except in parliamentarian-held areas in 1643–5 and some disturbed areas in 1659–60. But their records have not survived so well. See *List and Index Society* (vol. 6 1966), 'Clerks of Assize, Class List'. Many survive for the original western and northern circuit, some for the 'Oxford' or west Midlands, the 'Home' or south-eastern and the 'Norfolk' or East Anglian, and for the old Midland circuit. See however, the excellent records of the equivalent Court of Great Sessions at Chester, P.R.O., Chester 24, 127/1–130/4. For more background information, see J. S. Cockburn, *A History of English Assizes 1558–1714* (Cambridge, 1971). For a neglected aspect of the work of Quarter Sessions and Assizes, see J. S. Morrill, *The Cheshire Grand Jury 1625–1656: a social and administrative study* (1976), which includes a section on other counties.

There are many suits or cases with material of local interest in the records of the Courts of Chancery, Common Pleas, Exchequer and King's Bench (known as Upper Bench, 1649–60). For those years, as for the whole period up to the nineteenth century, the problem is to locate cases relating to any one county in voluminous, uncalendared collections. As a first step, consult the relevant volumes in P.R.O. *Lists and Indexes* and the *List and Index Society*. For some Chancery series, see also *Brit. Rec. Soc. Index Lib.* (vols 2, 5, 6, 14, 29, 32 and P.R.O. *Lists and Indexes*, vols xxx, xxix, xlii, xliv, xlv). The Patent Rolls (C66), one of the standard sources for official appointments, including those of local importance, are extremely fragmentary for these years. See R. B. Pugh, 'The Patent Rolls of the Interregnum', *B.I.H.R.*, XXIII (1950), pp. 178–81; the volumes of contemporary indexes are in the Long Room at the P.R.O. The lack of Patent Rolls may be partly made good with the help of the following: P.R.O.

Index 16,818, Index (contemporary) of Chancery Officers, now in the Long Room; W. H. Black, *Docquets of Letters Patent* (issued by Charles I at Oxford) . . . *1642-6* (printed but never published, 1837; 2-volume photocopy now in P.R.O., Round Room); *4th Rept. of Dep. Keeper of Public Records*, appendix II, Enrolment of Letters Patent at Oxford, 1643-6, and of Oliver and Richard Cromwell, 1654-9, and *ibid, 5th Rept.*, appendix II, continued 1655-60; P.R.O., C.181/6, Crown Office, Entry Book of Commissions; C.216/3, Chancery Admission Roll, 1655-6; Index 4213, Crown Office Docquet Book 1643-60; E.403/2523, Exchequer of Receipt, Enrolment Book, Pells, 1644-60; E.403/2608, Exchequer of Receipt, Privy Seal Book, Pells, 1655-60; B.M., Add. MS 4184, Signet Register, 1654-60; Stowe MS 497, Register of Letters Patent in the Treasury, 1654-9.

Many local appointments, especially for the years 1642-53, are contained in legislation and other parliamentary instruments. For legislation 1640-42, see *Statutes of the Realm* (large folio, 11 vols 1810-28, and reprinted 1963, vol. V); for 1642-60, (eds) C. H. Firth and R. S. Rait, *Acts and Ordinances of the Interregnum.* Vol. III contains a very full Index of Names, Places and Things, and a somewhat uneven one to Subjects, including some places (e.g. London, Westminster, York). Note also that the list of ordinances in vol. III includes some not printed in vols I-II, for which see the *Journals of the House of Lords,* vols IV-X, for 1642-8, and the *Journals of the House of Commons,* vols II-VII, a few for 1649-53. Other parliamentary material can be approached through the *H.M.C., 1st to 9th Repts*, appendices (below Appendix 1), M. F. Bond, *Guide to the Records of Parliament,* (H.M.S.O. 1971) and other occasional publications of the House of Lords Record Office. Besides the Journals of the two Houses, parliamentary diaries of debates and committees may also be helpful. For 1640-1 and 1641-2 (with a gap in between, see (ed.) W. Notestein, *The Journal of Sir Simonds D'Ewes* . . . (New Haven, Conn. 1923) and (ed.) W. H. Coates, the same (N.H. 1942)). Other printed diaries can be traced through Keeler and other Bibliographies. For 1646-7, see (ed.) M. F. Stieg, 'The Diary of John Harington', *Somerset Rec. Soc.,* vol. 74 (1977), and for 1647-8, see (ed.) D. E. Underdown, 'The Parliamentary Diary of John Boys . . .' *B.I.H.R.,* XXXIX (1966). For other diaries and autobiographical pieces with parliamentary material during the years 1642-8, it is necessary to go straight to the originals, namely: B. M., Harl. MSS 162-6 (the rest of D'Ewes);

Add. MSS 18, 780 (Walter Yonge – very difficult to decipher); Add. MSS 31, 116 (Laurence Whitaker); Add. MSS 37, 343–5 (Bulstrode Whitelock's 'Annals', which are more useful for this purpose than his published *Memorials*). For the parliaments of 1654–9, there is (ed.) J. T. Rutt, *Diary of Thomas Burton* ... (4 vols 1828, reprinted 1972), that for 1654 being in fact from the manuscript of Guibon Goddard. There are no diaries for the Rump, the Barebones, or the resumed Rump Parliament of 1659–60. Much parliamentary material is also to be found in the newsbooks in the Thomason collection. For a discussion of the newspapers in the early 1650s, see A. B. Worden, *The Rump Parliament* (1973), chapter 1.

For the executive side of central government in relation to local affairs see (ed.) R. R. Steele, *A Bibliography of Proclamations* ... *1485–1714*, vol. I England & Wales (being Part V of *Bibliotheca Lindesiana* (Oxford 1910)), and – above all – the State Papers in the P.R.O. First, for what is printed, see above, pp. 6–9, and below, Appendix 2.

The most important of the near-contemporary compilations from original sources, not all of which are still otherwise available, is John Rushworth's *Historical Collections* (4 parts in 7 vols 1659–1701; 2nd edition 1721), of which vols IV–VII cover November 1640 to January 1649. The rival collection by the Anglican-Royalist John Nalson, *An Impartial Collection* ... (2 vols 1682–3) only reached January 1642, but the documents collected for its continuations are calendared in *H.M.C., 13th Report, Portland*, vol. I. The Lenthall Papers (Bodl. Lib., Tanner MSS 66–51) contain as many letters relating to local affairs (particularly military and administrative matters) as do the State Papers Domestic, and are as important. William Lenthall was Speaker of the House of Commons throughout the Long Parliament and the Rump.

For the 1650s, these collections are matched by the *Thurloe State Papers*, (ed.) T. Birch, 7 vols 1742; this is not a calendar but a full edition. However, readers are warned that it is frequently inaccurate, particularly in the transcription of names of people and places. It is fullest for the Protectorate, December 1653 to April 1659; for the unpublished part of the collection, see the Bodleian *Catalogue* ... *Rawlinson* (Oxford, 1862), Fasciculus I, for Part A of the Rawlinson MSS, helpfully marked to show which are printed in Birch. Amongst other recent editions or collections (ed.) W. C. Abbott, *The Writings and Speeches of*

Oliver Cromwell (4 vols, Cambridge, Mass. 1937–47) and the *Calendar of the Clarendon State Papers* (5 vols, Oxford 1872–1970) are pre-eminent.

There is less of local interest in the papers, published or unpublished of other leading figures. For example, Oliver's second son, Henry Cromwell (B. M., Lansdowne MSS 821–3), Edward Mountague, later Earl of Sandwich (Bodl., Carte MSS 73–5, 103, 223, 274), Edward Nicholas, royalist Secretary of State 1641–62 (ed.) G. F. Warner, 'The Nicholas Papers', 4 vols. *Camden Soc.*, new ser. 40, 50, 57, and 3rd ser. 31 (1886–1920), and unpublished items in B. M. Egerton MSS 2533–62 and Add. MSS 4180; another part of the Nicholas papers was published as an appendix to vol. IV of (ed.) W. Bray, *Diary and Correspondence of John Evelyn* (4 vols 1854), the most accessible of several editions; (ed.) J. Nicholls, *Original Letters & Papers of State addressed to Oliver Cromwell . . . 1649–58* (1743), generally known as the *Milton State Papers,* the originals of which have since disappeared. Apart from Bulstrode Whitelocke (see above) and Edmund Ludlow (see below), the leading political figures among the parliamentarians of the 1640s and the republicans of the 1650s are conspicuous for not having left any substantial collections of papers – with or without local materials. The papers of William Clarke, who followed Rushworth as an Army Secretary, (ed.) C. H. Firth, 'The Clarke Papers . . .' (4 vols, *Camden Soc.*, new ser. 49, 54, 61–2. 1891–1901), are mainly of value for the Army (see below) and for affairs in Scotland; there is a brief typed list of the collection, of which there is now a Harvester Press microfilm edition, by G. E. Aylmer in the Library at Worcester College, Oxford, to which inquiries should be addressed. On the royalist side, the Privy Council Registers are available (in reduced facsimile) down to 1645 but they are very thin indeed after September 1640 (see P.R.O., *Privy Council Registers: Facsimiles* (vols VIII–XI cover November 1639–September 1640, vol. XII covers October 1640–August 1645).

The other main series of royalist civil war records are the Ordnance Papers, recently edited in two volumes by Ian Roy, *Oxfordshire Rec. Soc.*, 43, 49 (1964, 1974). But much incidental light is shed on royalist administration in the letter books of Prince Rupert, B.M. Add MSS 18980–3 (a generous selection of which appears in E. Warburton, *Memorials of Prince Rupert and the Cavaliers,* 3 vols 1849) and in the letter books of Edward

Walker, strongest for the West Country and South Wales (B.M. Harl. MSS 6802-4, 6851). The order book of the commissioners of array for Glamorganshire is probably the only example of its kind (Nat. Lib. Wales, Diocese of Llandaff Records, LL/MB/17. An edition is appended to the thesis by Thomas listed in Appendix 8, no. 16). An excellent collection of local materials relating to royalist local government appears in (ed.), J. W. Willis-Bund, 'The Diary of Henry Townshend of Elmley Lovett', *Worcs. Hist. Soc.* (2 vols 1916, 1920).

4. Local Politics

The identification of individual royalists and parliamentarians is not as easy as it might seem. The principal source for royalists is the *Cal. of the Comm. for Compounding,* vols 1 and 5 of which contain sound and useful introductions. The first part of vol. 1 is taken up with a calendar of the letter books of the central committee, and includes lists of all those under sequestration for royalism in specified areas on particular dates. The bulk of the calendar is biographically organised, all the papers relating to each family being listed together. By thumbing through the 3,000-plus pages a complete list of those *treated as royalists* in any particular county can be made (the index of places is very unreliable). But even these lists will exclude references to many men whose lands were sequestered but who never entered into negotiations to regain their lands by paying fines. References to such men can be tracked down only in the uncalendared letter books of the Committee of Sequestrations (SP20) or in the Rump's three Acts of Sale of the lands of those excluded from the right to compound (Firth and Rait, *op. cit.*). A national list of delinquents has been published by M. G. W. Peacock in the *Index Society* (1879). Calendars of composition papers have appeared for the counties of Durham, Lancashire, Northumberland and Yorkshire (for details see the work of Mullins noticed in Appendix I, item 8, p. 568). Other important series of records relating to sequestrations are in the B.M. Add. MSS 5478, 5491, 5494, 5497, 5501, 5505, 5508, 8845, 16178. But there are all kinds of problems about using these records as evidence of royalism, and even more about using them as evidence of the wealth of royalist families. See such works as those given in Appendixes 7 and 8. An article by R. N. Dore and J. S. Morrill, 'The Allegiance of the Cheshire Gentry in the Great Civil War',

Trans Lancs & Cheshire Antiq. Soc., 1967 concentrates on the problems of using these sources.

Parliamentarians are even more difficult to identify. Even the list of committee men in Firth and Rait (*op. cit.*) only say who was appointed (many can be shown not to have served: others may also have refused). But the papers of the Indemnity Committee (P.R.O., SP24) are a neglected source. This committee (established in May 1647) was empowered to indemnify against actions in the normal courts all those who had acted under the orders of Parliament, in either a military or civilian capacity. The order books of the committee contain a contemporary index of causes and suits (by plaintiffs and petitioners), and the loose papers are arranged alphabetically in the same way (see *Lists and Indexes*, vol. 43). Similarly those who rummage in the brantub of SP28 (*Lists and Indexes, Supplementary* vol. 10), in the boxes listed as containing the accounts for particular counties, will come up with a reward for their dusty efforts.

For the divisions between the two sides and their local ramifications, most detailed work has been done on M.P.s. The Long Parliament has been served particularly well. See (in order of publication) D. Brunton and D. H. Pennington, *Members of the Long Parliament* (1954, reprinted 1968); M. F. Keeler, *The Long Parliament 1640–1*, (American Phil. Soc., Philadelphia 1954); D. E. Underdown, *Pride's Purge: Politics in the Puritan Revolution* (Oxford 1971); J. R. MacCormack, *Revolutionary Politics in the Long Parliament* (Harvard 1973) – eccentric in its political 'labels' and less reliable than Underdown; A. B. Worden, *The Rump Parliament 1648–1653* (Cambridge 1974). There is nothing comparable yet for Barebones or the Protectorate Parliaments, except for a good unpublished American thesis by P. J. Pinckney, 'A Cromwellian Parliament: The Elections and Personnel of 1656' (Univ. of Vanderbilt Ph.D. thesis, 1962), from which comes a model article on 'The Cheshire Elections of 1656', *Bull. of the J. Rylands Lib.* vol. 49 (1967). For the political behaviour of members of the House of Lords, see C. H. Firth, *The House of Lords during the Civil Wars* (1910 repr. 1975) and (despite its title) L. Stone, *The Crisis of the Aristocracy 1558–1641* (Oxford 1965).

There are a few contemporary and modern estimates of how the gentry divided on a county basis (for example, for Derbyshire see *C.S.P. Dom. 1661–2*, p. 613; for Staffordshire (ed.) R. M. Kitson 'The Gentry of Staffordshire, 1662–3', *Collections for a History of Staffordshire*, 4th series, vol. 2 (1958); for Yorkshire, J. T. Cliffe, *The Yorkshire Gentry* (1966), and J. W. Clay 'The Gentry of Yorkshire at the time of the civil war', *Yorks. Arch. Jnl*, XXIII (1905); for Lancashire, B. G. Blackwood 'The Cavalier and Roundhead Gentry of Lancashire', *T. Lancs & Chesh. Antiq. Soc.*, 117 (1967)). For discussions of the divisions within the gentry, see also G. E. Aylmer, *The King's Servants 1625–42* (1961) and *The State's Servants, 1649–1660* (1974) which are partly biographical in approach and which attempt to relate the officials of the central government to their localities. See also below, Appendix 7, nos 21, 25, 29 and Appendix 8, nos 1, 6, 10, 11, 14.

For committee disputes and local reactions to the political developments of the 1640s and 1650s, the sources are the same as for section 3 above. Here above all, the researcher will be dependent upon the chance survival of private family correspondence for the period, which may be in the British Library, the local record office or private hands. The Thomason Tracts in the British Library (above, p. 11) should also be explored. Sometimes gentlemen or factions denounced the politics of their local enemies in print (e.g. for Lincolnshire, Colonel Edward King's *A Discovery of the Tyrannical and Illegal Actions of Some of the Committees of the County of Lincoln* or, for Somerset, Humphrey Willis' *Times Whirligig or the Blew-New-Made Gentleman Mounted*, both 1646). Such items can be found by a careful scrutiny of the Thomason catalogue (Appendix 1, item 13). But much interesting local news can only be found in the newspapers, and since the catalogue only gives the call number of each copy of a newspaper without any note on the contents, there is nothing for it but to call up samples for likely weeks and months. This will be rewarded by the likelihood of finding many amusing and illuminating digressions.

5. Warfare and the Armies

The older county studies come into their own here. Many of them have never been superseded. Anyone interested in reconstructing military activity in a particular vicinity should start with these volumes (traceable through Appendix 1, items 7 to 10). The fullest recent synthesis of military events is P. Young and R. Holmes, *The English Civil War* (though this perpetuates errors from Young's earlier work already pointed out by others). C. V. Wedgwood's *The King's War 1641-7* is less systematic as an account but does show how far military events depended on political and administrative developments, a point rather brushed aside by the military purists. Young and Holmes' book contains a good bibliography.

Those interested in the parliamentary armies should start with C. H. Firth's *Cromwell's Army* (1902, repr. 1962) and then turn to C. H. Firth and G. Davies, *The Regimental History of Cromwell's Army* (2 vols Oxford 1940), which covers the period 1645-60. For the army lists of both sides at the outset, see E. Peacock, *The Army Lists of Roundheads and Cavaliers* (1863; 2nd edn with index 1875). P. Young and W. Embleton, *The Cavalier Army* (1974) is a useful guide to royalist military organisations (a major work on this subject by I. Roy is to be published shortly), but Young and Embleton are no match for Firth and Davies.

In reconstructing the campaigns themselves, the essential sources are those already referred to in earlier sections: for the parliamentarians, the State Papers Domestic, the Lenthall Papers (extracts printed in (ed.) H. Cary, *Memorials of the English Civil War* (2 vols 1842)) and the Fairfax Papers (B.M., Add. MSS 18978-9, Sloane MSS 1719) partially printed in (ed.) R. Bell, *Memorials of the Civil War, comprising the Correspondence of the Fairfax Family* (2 vols 1819); for the royalists, the Rupert MSS (B.M. Add. MSS 18980-3) many printed in E. Warburton, *Memoirs of Prince Rupert and the Cavaliers* (3 vols 1849), *Cal. Clarendon State Papers* (above p. 12), and the papers of Edward Walker (B.M. Harl. MSS 6802-4, 6851). Above all, those interested in campaigns should explore the *Catalogue of the Thomason Tracts*, either exploiting the chronological format, or proceeding via the indexes. Once again, the diurnals contain as much information as do individual pamphlets (see also above, p. 11).

Many family collections are also full of important private letters and memoirs, and again the bibliographical guides in Appendix 1 should be consulted. Amongst the major collections which throw light on military affairs are the letter books of Sir William Brereton (B.M. Add. MSS 11311-13; Birmingham Public Lib., reference 595611; and a recently discovered volume for late 1644 still in private hands: photocopy in Cheshire Record Office) for the north midlands and Wales. The first three are being edited by R. N. Dore for the *Lancs and Cheshire Rec. Soc.*

in conjunction with the *H.M.C.* The letter books of Sir Samuel Luke, (ed.) H. G. Tibbutt, *H.M.C.* (JP 4) are useful for Bedfordshire, East Anglia and elsewhere; and the letter books of Basil, Earl of Denbigh, *H.M.C. 5th Report*, are useful for the west midlands. The publications of the Kineton Press over the past few years have shown what can be achieved by a close study of such sources and provide models for similar studies, e.g. P. Young, *Edgehill 1644* (1970) and *Marston Moor* (1972); P. Wenham, *The Great and Close Siege of York, 1644* (1970); J. Adair, *Cheriton 1644* (1974). Recent military biographies which throw light on the war in several counties include J. Adair, *Roundhead General* (1969), a study of Sir William Waller; F. T. R. Edgar, *Sir Ralph Hopton* (1968); V. Snow, *Essex the Rebel* (Nebraska, 1971).

The Commonwealth Exchequer Papers (P.R.O. SP 28 – see Appendix 2) contain a vast amount of material for studying the organisations and deployment of parliamentarian and republican armies: pay and conditions of service, use of free quarter, and the acquisition and distribution of weapons and ammunitions and other supplies. For a brilliant example of how to use these difficult sources, see C. Holmes, *The Eastern Associations 1642–6* (Cambridge 1974). For some comments on the inadequacies of pay and of the commissariat, see J. S. Morrill, 'Mutiny and Discontent in English Provincial Armies', *Past and Present* (no. 56, 1972), and I. Gentles, 'The Arrears of Pay of the Parliamentary Army at the end of the First Civil War', *B.I.H.R.* (vol. 48, 1975). For some printed military accounts, see (eds) E. Kitson and E. K. Clark 'Some Civil War Accounts 1647–1650', *Thoresby Soc.* (vol. XI, 1900–4). There is a nineteenth-century transcript of the fragmentary order book of the Northern brigade for 1647–8 in York Minster Library, MS Box BB53. But the logistics of war have yet to be properly studied for most counties and this is a topic handled poorly even in the best county studies.

6. Ecclesiastical History

The sources here are at once voluminous, in some cases distinctive, and often quite tricky to use. Much of the best work by modern historians is only of indirect relevance to the student of a particular locality: e.g. general studies and interpretations, however excellent, of Puritanism and other religious movements.

The church courts virtually ceased to function from 1641, and completely so within a few years of this, and did not start up again until 1660. Some of their regulatory work, in matrimonial cases etc., was taken over by the JPs in Quarter Sessions from 1646 or so onwards. But there was certainly variation here from one county to another. One area of their work was fully centralised from 1652 to 1660, namely all probate of wills and other testamentary business, under the Probate Judges in London. (see above, pp. 13–14). From 1642 to 1648 much energy was expended in helping clergy of whom Parliament approved, and proceeding against those of whom it disapproved. For the former category, if they survived into the 1660s and were then dispossessed or resigned, see A. G. Matthews, *Calamy Revised* (Oxford. 1934); for the latter – basically those who were dispossessed or who resigned in the 1640s, see A. G. Matthews, *Walker Revised*; *The Sufferings of the Clergy* (Oxford 1948). But there were of course other categories of clergy: those who held livings before 1642 and retained them, dying either during the interregnum or – in a few cases – surviving it, and those who only took up livings after 1642 but either died before 1660 or retained their livings in the 1660s. These are not covered by Calamy or Walker, or only incidentally so. For episcopalians and the measures taken against them, see the records of the so-called Committees for Scandalous Ministers: B.M., Add. MSS. 15, 672 (Cambridgeshire); Add. MSS. 5,829 (Essex); J. W. F. Hill, 'The Royalist Clergy of Lincoln', *Lincs. Architectural & Archaeolog. Soc. Repts.*, n.s. (vol. II 1938–9); and (ed.) C. Holmes 'Suffolk Committee . . . 1644–6', *Suffk. Rec. Soc.* (vol. XIII 1970). There is also information about these clergy, as well as about those instituted in their place and about others of whom Parliament approved, in the various papers of the 'Plundered Ministers' Committee': P.R.O., SP22, and a few items in SP28; B.M. Add. MSS. 15669–71; Bodleian MSS. 322–9. These records are available in print for Lancashire and Cheshire, (ed.) W. A. Shaw, *Lancs. & Chesh. Rec. Soc.*, 28 and 34 (1893, 1896). For institutions to livings and clergy holding benefices during the 1640s–50s, see P.R.O., E.339, Returns of Benefices & Incumbents, 1651–8, covering fourteen English and five Welsh counties (Index in Round Room) including retrospective information about the position in the later 1640s. And for the materials at Lambeth, see Houston (Appendix 1, no. 18), pp. 1–64 and Index of Persons. For an example of what can be done for one county, over a longer time-span, see G. D. Squibb, *Dorset Incumbents, 1542–1731* (n.d., but ?1954) reprinted from *Procs. of Dorset Nat. Hist. & Arch. Soc.* (vols 70–5, 1948–53). H. Smith, *The Ecclesiastical History of Essex under the Long Parliament and Commonwealth* (Colchester 1932) is ill organised, but prints useful documents both for the clergy and for church property.

On the survival of ecclesiastical records during and after this period, and the reasons why they survive where and in the form that they do, see the following: Dorothy M. Owen, 'Canterbury Archiepiscopal Archives in Lambeth Palace Library', *Jnl. of the Soc. of Archivists* (vol. II 1960–4), pp. 140–7; and 'Bringing Home the Records: the Recovery of the Ely Church Muniments at the Restoration', *Archives* (vol. VIII 1967–8), pp. 123–9; and C. J. Kitching, 'Probate during the Civil War and Interregnum', *Jnl. of the Soc. of Archivists* (vol. 5, nos 5–6, 1976). The fullest history of the Church as an institution, with many supporting documents, is still W. A. Shaw, *The English Church during the Civil Wars and under the Commonwealth,* 2 vols (1900). For the financial support of ministers (and teachers) in the 1650s, see also Houston (Appendix I, item 18), pp. 66–87. For the surviving records of the semi-Presbyterian structure of church organisation and government, set up by successive parliamentary Ordinances of 1645–8 and modified but never fully replaced by the changes of 1649 to 1654, see (besides Shaw's *English Church*), (ed.) W. A. Shaw, 'Minutes of the Bury Presbyterian Classis . . . 1647–57' *Chetham Soc.,* n.s., 36 and 41 (1896, 1898), vol. II containing also some records for Nottingham, Cornwall and Cambridge in the later 1650s; Shaw, 'Minutes of the Manchester Classis', *Chetham Soc.,* n.s., 20, 22, 24 (1890–1); (ed.) C. E. Surman 'Register Booke of the 4th Classis of London, 1646–59', *Harleian Society Registers* (vols 82–3, 1953). For relations between the national Church and the separatist churches, see also a short recent survey by Claire Cross in (ed.) Aylmer, *The Interregnum,* with bibliography; or now C. Cross, *Church and People 1450–1660* (1977). The literature, biographical and other, on early Nonconformity is vast, but much is focused on the fate of Puritan clergy and laymen after 1660, or is little more than hagiography; hence historical guides and interpreters who are both sympathetic but also discriminating are particularly important. Stephens (Appendix I, item 6), pp. 179–81 is full and clear. For catholics, here as over a much longer time-span, see the publications of the *Catholic Record Society.* There is some material, not published, in P.R.O., E.377, Recusant Rolls, for 1649–58. For recent approaches, see K. Lindley's chapter in (ed.) B. Manning, *Politics, Religion and the English Civil War* (1973), and J. Bossy, *The English Catholic Community 1570–1850* (1976). As in other respects, some counties are better served with accessible sources than others. See (ed.) M. Greenslade 'Staffordshire Recusants' – from a list compiled in 1657 – in *Collections for a Hist. of Staffs*, 4th series (vol. ii, 1958), pp. 71–100.

Some of the very best recent works by historians of the seventeenth century tend to cut across the traditional classifications of religious, social, even political and intellectual history. For two authors who have drawn, in different ways, on a wide range of local materials for works which are 'national' in scope, see Keith Thomas, *Religion and the Decline of Magic: Studies in Popular Beliefs in 16th and 17th Century England* (1972) and Christopher Hill, *The World Turned Upside Down: Radical Ideas during the English Revolution* (1972). See too sections or chapters in various histories of particular regions, counties, cities, towns, etc. (Appendices 7 and 8).

7. Education

Most of what can be said here, either as to sources or about modern secondary works, is to be found above relating to charities (section 2c) or religion (section 6). For an ambitious use of sources relevant for primary education, see Lawrence Stone, 'Literacy and Education in England 1640–1900', *Past & Present*, 42 (1969); but on this topic, see also R. S. Schofield's chapter in (ed.) J. Goody, *Literacy in Traditional Societies* (1968). W. A. L. Vincent, *The State & School Education in England & Wales, 1640–60* (1969), is a pioneering work based on printed sources and stronger on the grammar schools. Recent controversy about the intellectual state of the two English universities before, during and after the civil war and interregnum is hardly relevant for local history, save through the local origins and destinations of university students; on this there are no sources special to the years 1640–60. A few recent articles may show the way for further local and regional studies: A. J. Fletcher, 'The Expansion of Education in Berkshire & Oxfordshire, 1500–1670', *Brit. Jnl. Edcnl. Studs.* (vol. XV 1967); J. E. Stephens, 'Investment & Intervention in Education during the Interregnum', *ibid.*; S. M. Wide and J. A. Morris, 'Episcopal Licensing of Schoolmasters in the diocese of London, 1627–85, *Guildhall Miscellany* (vol. II 1967); A. M. d'I. Oakeshott, 'The Education Inquiry Papers of Christopher Wase', *Brit. Jnl. Edcnl. Studs* (vol. XIX 1971) – the Wase Papers contain retrospective material of relevance although the actual inquiry was made in the 1670s. Two valuable aids spanning the period are: Phyllis M. Jacobs, *Registers of the Universities, Colleges and Schools of Great Britain and Ireland: A List* (1964), also published in the *B.I.H.R.* (vol. XXXVII 1964), and P. J. Wallis, *Histories of Old Schools: A Revised List* . . . (Newcastle-upon-Tyne, 1966). The writing-schools, or 'secondary technicals' of their day, have so far been very poorly served by historians. See, for some pointers here, Ambrose Heal, *The English Writing-masters and their Copy-books, 1570–1800* (Cambridge 1931, reprinted Hildesheim 1962). Even the best served areas, historically speaking, have little for 1640–60: e.g. (ed.) B. Simon, *Education in Leicestershire: A Regional Study* (Leicester 1968). At present, the intellectual history of the interregnum is being largely rewritten by Charles Webster and others (see particularly, C. Webster *The Great Instauration* (1975) but there is still much more to be done on the local history of educational change.

8. Non-Literary Sources

One of the great strengths of the school of English local historians of the last thirty years or so has been their insistence on the need to combine close documentary study and field-work in a single discipline. The following elementary reminders may be helpful to the beginner in local history, as they have been over the years to the present authors, whose indebtedness to such scholars as Hoskins and Beresford will be obvious to anyone who has already done any work of this kind.

Funeral monuments and monumental inscriptions in churches and churchyards can often fill gaps in parish registers, genealogies and family histories. Beware, however, of upper-class families whose members suppressed mention of their parents' or other relatives' careers in the service of the Long Parliament and the Republic when erecting tombs after 1660! There are two such instances in York alone.

Without documentary corroboration, it is of course extremely difficult to date buildings within a period of twenty years on their appearance alone. As aids, a great deal can be done from the publications and the other records of the Royal Commission on Historic Monuments (23 Savile Row, London W1; also the National Monuments Record, at the same address); from the ex-L.C.C., now G.L.C., *Survey of London*, in progress 1900–, 37 volumes to date, general editor (since 1956) F. H. W. Sheppard; and – especially for areas not yet covered by the R.C.H.M. – from N. Pevsner and others, *The Buildings of England* (46 vols Harmondsworth 1951–74), an achievement worthy to rank with those of the great English topographers of the past – Leland, Camden and their like. See too the valuable study by M. W. Barley, *The English Farmhouse and Cottage* (1961), parts 3 and 4, besides Hoskins' famous article 'The Rebuilding of Rural England 1570–1640', originally in *Past & Present* no. 4 (1953), reprinted in his *Provincial England*. But see now R. Machin, 'The Great Rebuilding: a Reassessment,' *Past & Present* no. 77 (1977). Evidence of building, rebuilding, damage, alterations, etc, can often be verified from written sources, and the visual evidence can then tell one much more. Iconoclasm and other damage to churches is liable to be ascribed to the wrong Cromwell (Oliver instead of Thomas, or vice versa), or wrongly to either of them, in popular parish histories, church notes, and so on.

Paintings which show authentic scenes or individuals from the 1640s and 1650s are unfortunately very rare, except for portraits normally of the eminent. But prints, drawings and engravings, sometimes even early photographs, of any date before modern re-development, can be very helpful in cases where buildings or street layouts were altered little between the mid-seventeenth and the nineteenth century. For cities and towns which suffered from bad fires in the seventeenth century (not only London, but many smaller provincial towns, too) we are particularly dependent on such works, and – more obviously – on maps, plans, surveys and panoramas. These, especially maps and surveys, are helpfully discussed in Stephens and other general and bibliographical works already listed and in Appendix 1. To single out one contemporary seventeenth-century artist, the foreign-born Wenceslaus Hollar may not have been in the first rank as a draughtsman and illustrator, but he was an avid and, so far as we can tell, faithful recorder of what he saw; unluckily he left very little record of provincial England, aside from one or two somewhat untypical places like Windsor.

Tools, utensils, and other objects in local museums (or still in private hands) again can seldom be dated to within twenty years, though some like certain firebacks (collection in the Lewes Museum) have dates on them. Weapons and sometimes armour are, for obvious reasons, more easily dateable to the 1640s and 1650s, likewise coins and medals. Evidence of battles is still – literally – to be found on the ground or just under its surface in some places, in the form of musket balls and even human bones; there are spectacular earthworks at Newark-on-Trent, well described in an R.C.H.M. volume. Parts of the Oxford defences can also be followed by the observant visitor. The Committee of Aerial Photography at Cambridge University has a great deal of experience in these matters and holds a large store of photographs of civil war earthworks, field systems, etc. The director, Professor J. K. St Joseph, will be happy to help anyone who gets in touch with him.

But it is not only for battles and buildings that field-work and documentary evidence should, wherever possible, be combined. The same applies to street plans, roadways, bridges, waterways, the extent of afforestation and woodland, land drainage, enclosure, and even mining operations and quarrying. Once more, unless there are written records also, it is most unlikely that any of these can be dated with sufficient accuracy to ascribe them to particular decades, however clearly visible the evidence of changes – from some date between the fourteenth and eighteenth centuries – may be on the ground, or from the air. W. G. Hoskins, *The Making of the English Landscape* (1955) and the volumes for individual counties or regions to which it has given rise, show splendidly what can be done.

Finally, although full of dangers for the naïve and unwary, oral tradition should not be completely overlooked. It is more likely nowadays to have been passed down in a family than in a district. And more often, even if any strictly oral traditions have become extinct during the last century or so, they may have been recorded in writing before that. Alternatively, traditions may still be extant and valuable, even if they do not go back more than a century or so. J. S. M. was given an account of a skirmish at Eynsham which made far more sense than a second-hand account written at the time. Proceed with caution but an open mind!

The mid-seventeenth century was a turbulent period in English history. The records reflect that turbulence. Much has been destroyed, much more that was transitory, expedient, untidy, has survived. This guide should serve both to indicate some of the *lacunae* in the evidence and also to offer hope of rich treasures in store for the resourceful student and searcher. We hope it is not intimidating. But we also hope that it has given you some sense of the vast amount of material still unused or underused. We are very conscious of the frustrations you are likely to encounter in following through your subjects. But we hope that the final impression you have gained from this pamphlet will be a positive one. As practitioners who have explored the highways and some of the byways of this period, we can assert that we have been refreshed more often than we have been exhausted by the experience! The traveller who journeys through the English provinces in the 1640s and 1650s is not in for a comfortable or a speedy trip: but he can look forward to many exhilarating moments and some surprises.

III Bibliographical Appendices

Appendix 1

General Aids

The following are the most basic guides.

1 W. E. Tate, *The Parish Chest* (1946, 3rd edn 1969); complemented by D. M. Owen, *Records of the Established Church in England excluding Parochial Records* (British Records Association, 'Archives and the User', no. 1, 1970).

2 F. W. Kuhlicke and F. G. Emmison, *English Local History Handlist* (Historical Association, 1947. Reissued as 'Helps for Students of History', series no. 69, 1965); and F. G. Emmison and I. Gray, *County Records* (Historical Association, 1948, reissued as 'Helps for Students of History', series no. 62, 1961).

3 R. B. Pugh, *How to Write a Parish History* (1954).

4 M. Beresford, *History on the Ground* (1957, revised edn 1971).

5 W. G. Hoskins, *Local History in England* (1959, 2nd edn 1972).

6 W. B. Stephens, *Sources for English Local History* (1973).

General Guides to Printed Material

7 (ed.) M. F. Keeler (revising (ed.) G. Davies), *Bibliography of British History, Stuart Period* (1970). (Look at more than section XI on local history.)

8 (ed.) E. L. C. Mullins, *Texts and Calendars: An Analytical Guide to Serial Publications* (Royal Hist. Soc., 'Guides and Handbooks', no. 7, 1958). Supplement in progress.

9 (eds) A. T. Milne and others, *Writings on British History 1901–1933*; and annual volumes for 1934 on (1937 forward). These are divided into periods and from 1934 on the Tudor-Stuart volumes or sections of volumes include articles from

local journals and editions of sources. The gap left for 1901–33 in this respect is covered by:

10 E. L. C. Mullins, *Guide to the Historical and Archaeological Publications of Societies in England and Wales 1901–1933* (Inst. of Hist. Research, 1968).

11 D. G. Wing, *Short-Title Catalogue of Books printed in England, Scotland, Ireland, Wales and British America and of English books printed in other countries, 1641–1700*, 3 vols (New York, 1945–1951), vol I ('A–E' 2nd edn 1972).

More Specialised Catalogues

12 *The British Museum: General Catalogue of Printed Books* (263 vols 1960–6: contains everything printed up to 1954: five and ten-year supplements are appearing).

13 G. K. Fortescue and others, *Catalogue of the Pamphlets, Books, Newspapers and Manuscripts collected by George Thomason 1640–1661*, 2 vols (1908).

14 (comp.) T. R. Thomson, *A Catalogue of British Family Histories* (1935, 3rd edn 1976).

15 W. Matthews, *British Diaries written between 1442 and 1942* (1960).

16 W. Matthews, *British Autobiographies* (1956).

17 W. C. Abbott, *Bibliography of Oliver Cromwell* (1929). (Supplement by P. H. Hardacre, covering 1929–60 in *J.M.H.* 33, 1961.

18 J. Houston, *Catalogue of Ecclesiastical Records of the Commonwealth 1643–1660 in the Lambeth Palace Library* (1968).

19 M. F. Bond, *House of Lords Record Office: Guide to the Records of Parliament* (1971).

20 B. J. Steel, *National Index of Parish Registers* (1968 forward).

21 J. S. W. Gibson, *Wills and Where to Find Them* (1974).

22 M. W. Barley, *A Guide to British Topographical Collections* (1974).

Special Sources

Since the late nineteenth century, the Historical Manuscripts Commission had not only advised many private and corporate owners of historical manuscripts on the care and protection of their collections but has also published lists and calendars of very many major collections. The Commission's Reports now run into hundreds of volumes which are fairly widely available throughout the country. There is no general guide, except for the recent *Guide to the Reports Published 1911–1971, Part I, Index of Places* (ed.) A. C. J. Hall, which unhappily is very awkward to use.

Any selection within the H.M.C. is bound to be arbitrary and to omit valuable items. Among the volumes which include material on the years 1640–60 of potential local interest are the following: nos 1–8, Appendices to *Reports I* to *IX*; no. 9, *Salisbury (Cecil) at Hatfield*, vol XXII; 11, *Gawdy*; 12, *Wells*; 13, *Westmorland, etc.*; 15, *Abergavenny, etc.*; 17, *House of Lords*, new ser., XI; 22, *Leeds, etc.*; 23, *Cowper, II–III*; 24, *Rutland*, II and IV; 25, *Le Fleming;* 27, *Beaufort, etc.;* 29, *Portland, I–III, VIII*; 31, *Loder Symonds, etc.;* 33, *Lonsdale;* 35, *Kenyon;* 37, *Lincoln, etc.;* 38, *Buckinghamshire, etc.;* 39, *Hodgkin;* 43, *Somerset, etc.;* 45, *Buccleugh (at Montagu House), I, III*; 51, *Leyborne-Popham;* 52, *Frankland-Russell-Astley (formerly at Chequers);* 53, *Montague of Beaulieu;* 55, *Various*, esp. I, II, IV, VII, VIII; 58, *Bath*, II, IV; 62, *Lothian;* 63, *Egmont*, I; 64, *Verulam;* 66, *Ancaster;* 68, *Denbigh*, V; 69, *Middleton;* 70, *Pepys;* 71, *Finch*, I; 73, *Exeter;* 77, *De L'Isle and Dudley*, VI; 78, *Hastings*, I, II, IV; Note also the Joint Publications series, the volumes in which can usually be located under the particular local society with which H.M.C. has co-operated, as well as under the Commission: e.g. *Luke* (J.P., 4), *Cinque Ports* (J.P., 5). In the absence of a subject-index, Eleanor S. Upton and George P. Winship, Jr, (eds), *Guide to Sources of English History from 1603 to 1660 in Reports of the Royal Commission on Historical Manuscripts* (Washington, D.C., 1952), which covers the first nine *Reports* and subsequent *Reports* on any of the same collections, is the best that we have.

Other guides, indexes and lists of particular importance for unpublished sources are held by the National Register of Archives (an integral part of the H.M.C., housed with it in Quality House, Quality Court, off Chancery Lane, London WC2). Although duplicated copies of its reports on collections listed are held by the copyright libraries and two or three others, there appears to be only one set north of Cambridge, south of Edinburgh, and east of Aberystwyth!

A visit is strongly recommended: the indexes of subjects and persons are not duplicated, and the latest reports are not always distributed. The N.R.A. reports do not cover public records, central or local, nor collections of documents already printed in full or in abbreviated, 'calendared' form. But they are invaluable for private papers, either still in private hands or deposited in local record offices and public libraries.

A Guide to the Main State Papers Series

For SP16 to SP27 series, see P.R.O., *Lists and Indexes*, 43.
The following series are calendared in the *Cal. State Papers Domestic, Charles I (1625–1649)* and *Interregnum 1649–60* – SP16, SP18, SP21, SP25.
The *Cal. Committee for Compounding* (5 vols) is a calendar of the SP23 series, the *Cal. Committee for the Advance of Money* (3 vols) is a calendar of the SP19 series.

SP16: State Papers Domestic for the reign of Charles I (mainly papers passing through the hands of the Secretaries of State); 541 volumes.

SP18: State Papers Domestic, Interregnum (working papers of the Councils of State 1649–59). Scattered amongst them are the papers of the Admiralty Committee and of the Commissioners for the Navy, 1649–59); 225 volumes.

SP19: The Papers of the Committee for the Advance of Money 1643–53 (which assessed and collected money from all men of substance who refused to lend voluntarily to Parliament in 1642–3); 165 volumes.

SP20: Papers of the Committee for Sequestrations, 1643–9 which administered the estates of those accused of having voluntarily helped the royalist cause or of being catholics and whose lands were thereby confiscated to the service of the state. When it was merged with the Committee for Compounding its working papers were absorbed by the new committee (SP23). The thirteen volumes are largely the order books of the committee and are an important and neglected source.

SP21: Papers of the Committee of Both Kingdoms (1644–7) and the Derby House Committee (1647–9). These were the principal executive committees of the Parliament; 29 volumes.

SP22: Papers of the Committee of Plundered Ministers, which assisted in finding livings for and augmenting the stipends of ministers loyal to Parliament (1645–53); 3 volumes.

SP23: Papers of the Committee of Compounding with Delinquents, 1643–59. Responsible for negotiating the conditions upon which the delinquents (royalists and catholics) regained their estates. Contains most of the papers of the Committee for Sequestrations; 266 volumes.

SP24: Papers of the Committee for Indemnity (1647–55), which granted protection to all civilian officials for actions undertaken upon ordinances of Parliament, and to all soldiers for things done in the time and place of war. The order books are in chronological order, the petitions in alphabetical order of supplicants; 87 volumes.

SP25: Order Books of the Councils of State (1649–59); 139 volumes.

SP26: Papers of the Trustees for Fee Farm Rents and of the Committee for Crown Lands during the years when Parliament was selling them off; 10 volumes.

For SP28 see *Lists and Indexes*, Suppl. series no. 10.

SP28: These are the so-called Commonwealth Exchequer Papers which are in fact a miscellany of documents which were artificially grouped together. Many of them are properly not State Papers but stray records from the King's Remembrancer papers of the Exchequer. Its existence is the responsibility of nineteenth-century archivists who consigned to this class most things they failed to accommodate elsewhere. The most important groups within the series are:

Vols 1–119, orders and warrants by the committee of the army and military commanders for payments to troops and contractors (1642–60), organised chronologically not geographically – no index.

Vols 120–5, muster rolls, arranged chronologically(1644–51).

Vols 126–139, military accounts (arranged county by county).

Vols 148–204, assessments, loans, contributions, etc., arranged county by county.

Vols 205–18, sequestration papers, arranged geographically.

Vols 219–251, papers of county committees, arranged geographically.

Vols 252–260, papers of the committee for taking the accounts of the kingdom.

Vols 271–7, papers of the Trustees for Sale of Crown lands.

(The remainder of the 350 volumes are truly miscellaneous.)

Printed Guides, Calendars, and Extracts from County Records

A

1 Bedfordshire: (ed.) W. Le Hardy and G. Page, 'Notes and Extracts from the County Records, being a calendar of vol. I of the Quarter Sessions Minute Books, 1651–1660', *Bedf. County Recs.* (vol. II n.d.).

2 Cheshire: (eds) J. H. E. Bennett and J. C. Dewhurst, 'Quarter Sessions Records 1559–1670', *Lancs and Chesh. Rec. Soc.*, 94 (1940), calendared extracts.

3 Derbyshire: (ed.) J. C. Cox, *Three Centuries of Derbyshire Annals* (1890), extracts.

4 Devon: (ed.) A. H. A. Hamilton, *Quarter Sessions from Queen Elizabeth to Queen Anne* (1878), selections only.

5 Essex: (ed.) D. H. Allen, 'Essex Quarter Sessions Order Book', *Essex R.O. Publications* (no. 65, 1974).

6 Hertfordshire: (ed.) W. J. Hardy, *Hertfordshire County Records* (vol. 1, 1905, vol 5, 1928, vol. 6, 1930), extracts from Q.S. rolls 1581–1698, and calendar of the Q.S. minutes book, 1619–57, 1658–1700.

7 Middlesex: (ed.) J. C. Jeafferson, *Middlesex County Records* (vol. 3, 1890), Q.S. extracts.

8 Norfolk: (ed.) E. Howell James, 'Quarter Sessions Order Book 1650–7', *Norfolk Rec. Soc.*, 27 (1955).

9 Northamptonshire: (ed.) J. Wake, 'Quarter Sessions Records . . . 1630, 1657–8', *Northants Rec. Soc.*, I (1924).

10 Nottinghamshire: (ed.) H. H. Copnall, *Notts County Records of the 17th Century Notes and Extracts* (1915).

11 Oxfordshire: (ed.) M. S. Gretton, 'Oxfordshire J.P.s in the 17th Century', *Oxon Rec. Soc.*, 16 (1934), extracts only.

12 Shropshire: (eds) R. Lloyd Kenyon, P. O. Wakeman, *Shropshire County Records* (vols 1–2), abstract of Q.S. orders, etc. 1638–1708.

13 Somerset: (i) (ed.) E. H. Bates Harbin, 'Quarter Sessions Rec. . . .', *Som. Rec. Soc.* 28 (1922), transcript for years

1646–60 but reputedly unreliable; (ii) (ed.) J. S. Cockburn, 'Somerset Assize Orders 1640–8', *Som. Rec. Soc.*, 71 (1971).

14 Surrey: (eds) H. Jenkinson and D. L. Powell, 'Quarter Sessions Records: the order book for 1659–1661 (etc.)', *Surrey Rec. Soc.*, 13 (1934).

15 Sussex: (ed.) B. C. Redwood, 'Quarter Sessions Order Book 1642–9', *Sussex Rec. Soc.*, 54 (1954).

16 Warwickshire: (eds) S. C. Ratcliffe and H. C. Johnson, *Warwicks County Records* (vols 2–4, 1936–8), Q.S. Order Books 1637–50, 1650–7, 1657–65.

17 Wiltshire: (ed.) B. H. Cunnington, *Records of the County of Wiltshire* (1932); *H.M.C., Various Collections* I (1901). Both are calandars of seventeenth-century Q.S. papers.

18 Worcestershire: (i) (ed.) J. W. Willis-Bund, 'Worcester County Records: Calendar of Q.S. Papers 1591–1643', *Worcs. H.S.*, II (2 parts, 1899–1900); (ii) (ed.) R. D. Hunt, 'Henry Townshend – "Notes on the Office of Justice of the Peace",' *Worcs. Hist. Soc.*, n.s. (vol. 5, 1967).

19 Yorkshire: (i) (ed.) J. C. Atkinson, 'Quarter Sessions Records, 1634–47, 1647–58, 1658–77', *North Riding Rec. Soc.* (vols 4–6, 1886–8); (ii) (ed.) J. Lister, 'West Riding Sessions Records', orders 1611–42, indictments 1637–42, *Yorks. Arch. Soc.*, 2nd series, 67 (1915).

B

Items 11, 15, 16 and 18(i) have introductions very useful to anyone working on the history of local government in this period.

C

Other counties with unpublished quarter sessions records surviving from the whole, or part, of the period include Cheshire, Essex, Kent, Lancashire, Staffordshire and the east and west ridings of Yorkshire. There may very well be others.

City and Borough Records

Basic General Bibliographical Books

1 (ed.) M. Weinbaum, *British Borough Charters 1307–1660* (1943).
2 C. Gross, *A Bibliography of British Municipal History* (2nd edn 1966); complemented by:
3 (eds) G. H. Martin and S. McIntyre, *A Bibliography of British and Irish Municipal History*, I (1972).

Calendars, Extracts and Transcripts

1 London: (eds) W. H. and H. C. Overall *Analytical Index to the . . . Remembrancia (1579–1664)* (1878).
2 Bedford: (ed.) G. Parsloe, 'The Minute Book of Bedford Corporation, 1647–64', *Bedf. Hist. Rec. Soc. Publicns.*, 26 (1949).
3 Beverley: (ed.) J. Dennett, 'Beverley Borough Records, 1575–1821', *Yorksh. Arch. Soc. Rec. Ser.*, 84 (1932).
4 Burford: (ed.) R. H. Gretton, *Burford Records* (1920).
5 Calne: (ed.) A. W. Mabbs, 'Guild Steward's Book . . . 1561–1688', *Wilts A. & N.H.S.*, Rec. Branch, 7 (1953).
6 Carlisle: (eds) R. S. Ferguson and W. Nanson, 'Some Municipal Records of . . . Carlisle', extracts only, *Cumbs and Westm. Antiq. & Nat. Hist. Soc.*, extra series IV (1887).
7 Coventry: (i) *H.M.C. 15th Report, Appendix X* (list); (ii) (ed.), J. C. Jeafferson, *A Calendar. . . (1869)*; (iii) (ed.), M. D. Harris, *Coventry Leet Books*, 4 vols (1907–13).
8 Chester: (ed.) M. J. Groombridge, 'Cal. of the Chester City Council Minutes', *Lancs and Chesh. Rec. Soc.*, 106 (1956).
9 Dorchester: (ed.) C. H. Mayo, *Municipal Records of the Borough of Dorchester* (1908).
10 Durham: (ed.) C. E. Whiting, 'Durham Civic Memorials: The Order Book of the Corporation . . . 1602–66', *Surtees Soc.* (vol. 160, 1952).
11 Exeter: *H.M.C.*, 73, *Report on the Records of the City of Exeter*.

12 Hull: (ed.) T. T. Wildridge, *Hull Letters, 1625–1646* (n.d. ?1886), extracts.

13 Gloucester: (i) (ed.) W. H. Stevenson, *Calendar of records . . .* (1893); (ii) *H.M.C., 12th Report, Appendix IX.*

14 High Wycombe: (ed.) R. W. Greaves, 'The First Ledger Book . . .,' *Bucks. Rec. Soc.*, 11 (1956).

15 King's Lynn: *H.M.C., 11th Report, Appendix III.*

16 Leicester: (ed.) H. Stocks, *Records of the Borough . . . 1603–88* (vol. IV, 1923).

17 Lewes: (ed.) L. Z. Salzman, 'The Town Book . . . 1543–1701', *Sussex Rec. Soc.*, 48 (1947).

18 Lincoln: *H.M.C., 14th Report, Appendix VIII.*

19 Liverpool: (ed.) G. Chandler, *Liverpool under Charles I* (1965).

20 Manchester: (i) (ed.) J.P. Earwaker, *The Court Leet Records of the Manor of Manchester*, vol. 3: *1618–41*, vol. 4: *1647–62* (1886–7); (ii) (ed.) J.P. Earwaker, *The Constables Accounts of the Manor of Manchester*, vol. 2: *1633–47*, and appendices, *1648–59* (1892).

21 Newcastle under Lyme: T. Pape, *Newcastle-under-Lyme in Tudor and in early Stuart Times* (1938), appendix I, pp. 303–35 (corporation minutes 1640–1660).

22 Newcastle upon Tyne: (ed.) M. H. Dodds, 'Extracts from the Council Minute Book 1639–1656', *The Publcns. of the N-u-Tyne Recs. Committee* I (1920).

23 Norwich: (eds) W. Hudson and J. C. Tingey, *The Records of the City of Norwich*, 2 vols (1906–10).

24 Nottingham: (ed.) W. T. Baker, *Records of the Borough . . .* (vol. 5, 1900).

25 Oxford: (eds) W. G. Hobson and H. E. Salter, 'Oxford Council Acts 1626–1665', *Oxford Hist. Soc.* 95 (1933).

26 Northampton: (eds) C. A. Markham and J. C. Cox, *Records of the Borough . . .*, 2 vols (1898).

27 Peterborough: (ed.) W. T. Mellows, 'Peterborough Local Administration 1541–1689', *Northants. Rec. Soc.*, 10 (1937).

28 Reading: (i) (ed.) J. M. Guilding, *Reading Records*, 4 vols (1892–6); (ii) *H.M.C. 11th Report, Appendix VII.*

29 Rye: *H.M.C., 13th Report, Appendix IV.*

30 Salford: (ed.) J. G. de T. Mandley, 'Portmote or Court leet records', *Chetham Soc.*, n.s. 46 (1902).

31 Shrewsbury: *H.M.C. 15th Report, Appendix X.*

32 Southampton: *H.M.C. 11th Report, Appendix III.*

33 Weymouth: (i) (ed.) H. J. Moule, *A Descriptive Catalogue*...
   (1883); (ii) (ed.) M. Weinstock, 'Weymouth and Melcombe
   Regis Minute Book 1625–1660', *Dorset Rec. Soc.* I (1964).
34 Worcester: (ed.) S. Bond, 'The Chamber Order Book . . .
   1602–1650', *Worcs. Hist. Soc.*, 8 (1974). A model edition.
   The problem here is that many of these rather inadequate
   editions conceal more records than they reveal. There is
   much to be done.

Addenda
 1 Abingdon: (ed.) B. Challenor, *Selections from the Municipal
   Records of the Borough* (1898).
 2 Maidstone: (ed). K. S. Martin, *Records of Maidstone:
   Selections from Documents* (1926).
 3 Portsmouth: (comp.) A. J. Wullis and (ed.) M. J. Hoad,
   'Borough Sessions Papers 1653–1688', *Portsmouth Rec. Ser.*
   (vol. 1, 1971).
 4 Shrewsbury: (ed.) G. Edwards, 'The Orders of the Corporation . . . 1571–1735', *Trans. Salop Arch. & N.H. Soc.*
   (1888).
 5 Windsor: (ed.) S. Bond, 'The First Hall Book of the Borough
   of New Windsor 1653–1725', *Windsor Borough Hist. Recs.*
   (vol. 1, 1968).

Appendix 5
Printed County Committee Papers

Bedfordshire: (ed.) P. Bell, *Bedf. Rec. Soc.* (vol. 49, 1970), sequestration business only, 1646–7.

Durham: (ed.) R. Welford, 'Records of the Committees for Compounding . . .', *Surtees Soc.* (vol. 111, 1905) (pp. 1–38 are the papers of the Durham sequestration committee. The rest of the volume is extracted from P.R.O. SP23, committee for compounding).

Dorset: (ed.) C. H. Mayo, *The Minute Book of the Dorset Standing Committee 1646–50* (1902).

Kent: (ed.) A. M. Everitt, Account Book of County Committee 1646–7, in 'A Seventeenth Century Miscellany', *Kent Records,* (vol. 17, 1960), pp. 115–152.

Lancashire: (ed.) W. A. Shaw, 'Plundered Ministers Accounts', *Lancs and Cheshire Rec. Soc.* (vols 28, 34, 1893, 1897), papers of committee for plundered ministers and maintenance trustees, 1643–54, 1650–60.

Staffordshire: (eds) D. H. Pennington and I. A. Roots, *The Committee at Stafford 1643–5* (1958).

Suffolk: (ed.) A. M. Everitt, 'Suffolk and the Great Rebellion', *Suffolk Rec. Soc.* (vol. 3, 1960), sections 1 and 2. (ed.) C. Holmes, 'Suffolk Committee of Scandalous Ministers', *Suffolk Rec. Soc.* (vol. 13, 1970).

York: (ed.) A. Raine, 'Proceedings of the Commonwealth Committee . . .', *Yorks Arch. Soc., Record Ser.* (vol. 118, 1953).

There are now several studies of the committees and their activities. See particularly those listed in Appendix 7, items, 2, 9, 11, 14, 21, 22, 24, 26, 31 and Appendix 8, items 4, 6, 7, 8, 12, 13, 14, 15. See also H. E. Bannard, 'The Committees of 1642–6', *Berks, Bucks and Oxon Jnl* (vol. 31, 1925) and A. M. Everitt, 'The County Committee of Kent in the Civil War', *Leic. Univ. Occ. Paper in Local H.* (no. 9, 1957).

Printed Church Surveys

This contains most of the parliamentary surveys of church property to have appeared in print. (Others might be found by a thorough search of the aids listed in Appendix 1, items 8 and 10.)

Cheshire: (ed.) H. Fishwick, 'Church Surveys 1649–1655', part I Parochial, part II Bishop, Dean and Chapter and Collegiate Church of Manchester, *Lancs and Cheshire Rec. Soc.* (vol. I, 1879).

Durham: (ed.) D. A. Kirby, 'Surveys . . .', *Surtees Society* (vols 183, 185, 1971, 1972).

Kent: (ed.) A. Hussey, 'Survey of Ford, 1647', *Archaeologia Cantiana*, 26 (1902).

Lancashire: as for Cheshire.

Middlesex: (ed.) C. E. B. Bowles, 'Surveys of Edmonton in 1650', *Middx and Herts Notes and Queries* (vol. 3, 1897); (ed.) W. Robinson, *History and Antiquities of Hackney*, 2 vols (1842–3), vol. 1, pp. 409–40; (ed.) S. J. Madge, 'Rural Middlesex under the Commonwealth', *London and Middlesex Archaeol. Soc., Trans.*, n.s. 4 (1922), pp. 273–312, 403–57; (ed.) C. L. Kingsford, *The Early History of Piccadilly* (1925).

Somerset: (ed.) W. E. Hodgson, 'Wells, Wellesley and Dulcote, 1649', *Wells Nat. Hist. and Arch. Soc. Annual Reports* (1913).

Surrey: (ed.) A. R. Bax, 'Surveys of Surrey', *Surrey Archaeol. Collections*, (vol. 17, 1902); (ed.) A. R. Bax 'Surveys of Guildford Castle . . .', *ibid.* (vol. 18, 1903); (ed.) M. S. Giuseppi, 'Surveys of Southwark . . .', *ibid.* (vol. 14, 1899); (ed.) W. H. Hart, 'Surveys of Richmond, Wimbledon and Nonsuch', *ibid.* (vol. 5, 1890); (ed.) S. W. Kershaw, 'Surrey Surveys from Lambeth Sources . . .', *ibid.* (vols 8 and 12, 1893, 1897); (ed.) S. J. Madge, 'Surrey Surveys . . .', *ibid.* (vol. 37, 1922).

Wiltshire: (ed.) E. J. Bodington, 'Church Survey of Wiltshire, 1649–50', *Wilts Arch. and Nat. Hist. Soc.* (vols 40–1, 1918–20).

Worcestershire: (eds) J. Cave and R. A. Cave, 'Surveys of the Lands of the Dean and Chapter of Worcester, 1649', *Worcs. Hist. Soc.* (1924).

Yorkshire: (ed.) T. S. Willan, 'Parliamentary Surveys of the North Riding', *Yorks. Arch. Jnl* (vol. 31, 1934).

Appendix 7
Recent Studies

The purpose of this list is to indicate some of the recent books and articles to have appeared mainly during the last ten years. It is specifically intended to supplement the lists in Keeler (Appendix I, item 7) but it is not exhaustive. It is suggested that each of these has something to say about the sources for the period and their use, as well as about particular localities. Many of them contain bibliographies.

1   E. Andriette, *Devon and Exeter in the Civil War* (1972).
2   G. E. Aylmer, 'Who was Ruling in Herefordshire, 1644–1662', *Trans. of the Woolhope Club*, vol. XL (1974).
3   A. L. Beier, 'Poor Relief in Warwickshire', *Past and Present*, no. 35 (1966).
4   B. G. Blackwood, 'The Lancashire Gentry and the Great Rebellion 1640–60', *Chetham Soc.*, 3rd ser., vol. XXV (1978).
5   C. H. Chalklin, *Seventeenth Century Kent* (1965).
6   P. Clark, *English Provincial Society from the Reformation to the Revolution: Religion, Politics and Society in Kent 1500–1640* (1977).
7   (eds) P. Clark and P. Slack, *Crisis and Order in English Towns 1500–1700* (1972).
8   (eds) P. Clark and P. Slack, *English Towns in Transition 1500–1700* (1976).
9   A. M. Everitt, *The Community of Kent and the Great Rebellion* (1966).
10   A. M. Everitt, *Change in the Provinces* (1970).
11   A. M. Everitt, *Suffolk during the Great Rebellion* (1960).
12   (ed.) A. M. Everitt, *Perspectives in English Urban History* (1974), chs 3 and 4.
13   J. P. Ferris, 'The Dorset Gentry in 1640', *Genealogists Magazine* (vol. 15, 1965).
14   A. Fletcher, *A County Community in Peace and War: Sussex 1600–1660* (1975).

15 G. C. F. Forster, 'The East Riding Justices of the Peace in the Seventeenth Century', *E. Yorks Local Hist. Soc.* (1973).

16 I. Gentles, 'The Sales of Crown Lands During the English Revolution', *Ec. H.R.* 2nd series (vol. 26, 1973).

17 H. J. Habakkuk, 'Landowners and the Civil War', *Ec. H.R.* 2nd series (vol. 18, 1965).

18 H. J. Habakkuk, 'The Parliamentary Army and Crown Lands', *Welsh Hist. Rev.* (vol. 3, 1966–7).

19 D. Hey, *An English Rural Community: Myddle under the Tudors and Stuarts* (1974), for a Shropshire village.

20 P. G. Holiday, 'Land Sales and Repurchases in Yorkshire after the Civil Wars', *Northern History* (vol. 5, 1970).

21 C. Holmes, *The Eastern Association in the English Civil War* (1974).

22 (ed.) C. Holmes, 'The Suffolk Committee for Scandalous Ministers 1644–1646', *Suffolk Rec. Soc.* (1970).

23 C. Holmes, 'Colonel King and Lincolnshire Politics 1642–8', *H.J.* (1973).

24 M. James, *Family, Lineage and Civil Society* (1974), for County Durham.

25 R. W. Ketton-Cremer, *Norfolk in the Civil War: A Portrait of a Society in Conflict* (1969).

26 J. S. Morrill, *Cheshire 1630–1660* (1974).

27 J. S. Morrill, *The Revolt of the Provinces* (1976).

28 J. S. Morrill, *The Cheshire Grand Jury, 1625–59: A Social and Administrative Study* (1976).

29 D. H. Pennington, 'The Accounts of the Kingdom', in (ed.) F. J. Fisher, *Essays . . in Honour of R. H. Tawney* (1961).

30 (eds) D. H. Pennington and K. Thomas, *Puritans and Revolutionaries: Essays in the 17th Century History presented to Christopher Hill* (1978). See chs by Grassby, Johnson, Pearl and Underdown.

31 C. B. Phillips, 'County Committees and Local Government in Cumberland and Westmorland, 1642–1660', *Northern History* (vol. V, 1970).

32 R. E. Sherwood, *Civil Strife in the Midlands 1642–51* (1974).

33 M. Spufford, *Contrasting Communities* (1974) for Cambridgeshire.

34 (ed.) W. B. Stephens, *A History of Congleton* (1970), ch. 3.

35 D. Underdown, *Somerset in the Civil War and Interregnum* (1973).

36 J. Walter and K. Wrightson, 'Dearth and Social Order in early Modern England', *Past & Present*, no. 71 (1976).
37 (ed.) G. Williams, *Glamorgan County History* (vol. IV, 1974), chapters by Thomas and Johnson.

Addenda

1 J. Broad, 'Gentry Finances and the Civil War: The Case of the Buckinghamshire Verneys', *Ec. H.R.*, 2nd ser. (XXXII, 1979), pp. 183–200.
2 J. T. Cliffe, *The Yorkshire Gentry from the Reformation to the Civil War* (1969) and 'The Royalist Composition Papers and the Landed Income of the Gentry: A Rejoinder', *Northern History* (XIV, 1978), pp. 164–8.
3 A. J. Fletcher, 'Petitioning and the Outbreak of the Civil War in Derbyshire', *Derbs. Arch. Jnl.* (XCIII, 1973), pp. 33–44.
4 G. C. F. Forster, 'County Government in Yorkshire during the Interregnum', *Northern Hist.* (XII, 1976), pp. 84–104.
5 G. Jaggar, 'Colonel Edward Whalley, His Regimental Officers and Crown Land . . . 1650 to the Restoration', *Norfolk Archaeology* (36, 1975), pp. 149–66.
6 J. S. Morrill, 'Approaches to the Local History of the Great Rebellion', *Northern Hist.* (XV, 1979).
7 P. R. Newman, 'Catholic Royalist Activists in the North, 1642–1646', *Recusant History* (14, 1977), pp. 26–38.
8 C. B. Phillips, 'The Royalist Composition Papers and the Landed Income of the Gentry: A Note of Warning from Cumbria', *Northern Hist.* (XIII, 1977), pp. 161–74, and 'The Royalist North: The Cumberland and Westmorland Gentry 1642–1660', *ibid.* (XIV, 1978), pp. 169–92.

Appendix 8

Theses

This is a selective list of unpublished theses, each of which contains a useful bibliography and will serve as a good example of a particular approach to local history.

1   B. G. Blackwood, *The Lancashire Gentry 1625–1660.* Univ. of Oxford D.Phil. thesis, 1973.

2   J. Broad, *Sir Ralph Verney and His Estates,* Univ. of Oxford. D.Phil. thesis, 1973.

3   I. Gentles, *The Debentures Market and Military Purchases of Crown Land,* Univ. of London Ph.D. thesis, 1969.

4   G. A. Harrison, *Royalist Organisation in Wiltshire 1642–6,* Univ. of London Ph.D. thesis, 1963.

5   P. G. Holiday, *Royalist Composition Fines and Land Sales in Yorkshire, 1643–1663,* Univ. of Leeds Ph.D. thesis, 1966.

6   A. M. Johnson, *Buckinghamshire 1640–1660,* Univ. of Wales M.A. thesis, 1963.

7   A. M. Johnson, *Some Aspects of the Political, Constitutional, Social and Economic History of the City of Chester, 1550–1662,* Univ. of Oxford D.Phil. thesis, 1971.

8   M. V. Jones, *A Political History of the Parliamentary Boroughs of Kent, 1642–1662,* Univ. of London Ph.D. thesis, 1967.

9   G. Lynch, *The Risings of the Clubmen in the English Civil War,* Univ. of Manchester M.A. thesis, 1973.

10   A. M. Morton-Thorpe, *The Gentry of Derbyshire 1640–1660,* Univ. of Leicester M.A. thesis, 1971.

11   P. R. Newman, *The Royalist Armies in Northern England 1642–45,* Univ. of York D. Phil. thesis, 2 vols, 1978.

12   C. B. Phillips, *The Gentry of Cumberland and Westmorland, 1600–1665,* Univ. of Lancaster Ph.D. thesis, 1974.

13   J. T. Pickles, *Studies in Royalism in the English Civil War,* Univ. of Manchester M.A. thesis, 1968 (mainly on Staffordshire).

14   B. Quintrell, *The Divisional Committee of Southern Essex 1642–6,* Univ. of Manchester M.A. thesis, 1962.

15 R. H. Silcock, *County Government in Worcestershire, 1600–1660*, Univ. of London Ph.D. thesis, 1934.
16 C. M. Thomas, *The First Civil War in Glamorganshire*, Univ. of Wales M.A. thesis, 1963 (includes a transcript of the Commissioners of Array order book).
17 M. D. G. Wanklyn, *The King's Armies in the West of England*, Univ. of Manchester M.A. thesis, 1966.
18 K. E. Wrightson, *The Puritan Reformation of Manners, 1600–1660, with special reference to Lancashire and Essex*, Univ. of Cambridge Ph.D. thesis, 1974.